Cottage Ware

Ceramic Tableware Shaped as Buildings, 1920s-1990s

Eileen Rose Busby

Schiffer Publishing Ltd
4880 Lower Valley Road, Atglen, PA 19310 USA

Dedication

To Richard, my late husband, traveling partner, and best friend, who shared the fun (and the work) of the search for cottage and village pieces.
To my kids: Michael, Sally, Jon, Cordelia, and Cathy. and to my step-kids Nancy and Chuck.

Front cover. *Top, left to right*: Block canister #31, Biscuit barrel #314.
Center: Royal Winton covered jam on tray #281, Royal Winton covered cheese #296, Treasure Craft teapot #326.
Bottom: Delft container #68, Kensington double jam # 189, Japan covered jam #95.

Title page. *Courtesy of Shirley and Klaus Mendenhall*

Library of Congress Catalog Control Number: 2002113978

Designed by John P. Cheek
Cover design by Bruce M. Waters
Type set in Windsor BT/Souvenir Lt BT

ISBN: 0-7643-1745-8
Printed in China
1 2 3 4

Published by Schiffer Publishing Ltd.
4880 Lower Valley Road
Atglen, PA 19310
Phone: (610) 593-1777; Fax: (610) 593-2002
E-mail: Schifferbk@aol.com
Please visit our web site catalog at
www.schifferbooks.com
We are always looking for people to write books on new and related subjects. If you have an idea for a book, please contact us at the above address.

This book may be purchased from the publisher. Include $3.95 for shipping. Please try your bookstore first.
You may write for a free catalog.

In Europe, Schiffer books are distributed by
Bushwood Books
6 Marksbury Ave. Kew Gardens
Surrey TW9 4JF England
Phone: 44 (0)20 8392-8585; Fax: 44 (0)20 8392-9876
E-mail: Bushwd@aol.com
Free postage in the UK. Europe: air mail at cost.
Please try your bookstore first.

Contents

Acknowledgments

Many thanks to our many friends, collectors, and dealers in England, Canada, and various parts of the United States, who have been so helpful in finding information and appropriate pieces for this book.

Thanks to Frances and Brian Rothery, from England, for their gracious hospitality, encouragement, and helping my search for special cottage pieces.

To Reg and May Bladen, from England, for their hospitality and helpful anecdotes about growing up in the potteries, for the pot bank replica, and for locating old publications for me.

To Rosemary and Bob Karr, from Oregon, and to Shirley and Klaus Mendenhall, from San Diego, for sharing their collections and giving me display ideas.

To Ken Glibbery, International Royal Winton Chintz Collectors Club, Dancers End, Northall, Bedfordshire, England LU6 2EU, for kind permission to use the Royal Winton illustration.

To Anthony Wood, chairman of Price Kensington, Stoke-on-Trent, Staffordshire, England, for kind permission to use the Cottage Ware page from their catalog.

And finally, to David Richardson for his photographic skills.

Evergreen Hall, a 16th century thatched roof cottage in the center of Barningham, a small village in Suffolk, England. Richard and Eileen Busby owned and lived in the cottage from 1976 to 1978.

Preface

A brief history of each pottery that made cottage ware, and examples, are included in this book. Examples from distributors or those produced only for a special occasion or for advertising purposes may be listed under the distributor's name. Advertising is a category of its own. Back stamps from the pieces are included for identification purposes.

A price guide is exactly that, a fluctuating guide of prices found, not an absolute. It is not meant to be treated as though it were a catalog with exact prices. Prices are affected by many things: depth of color (has it faded?), rarity, demand, price paid by the dealer, and especially, age and condition of the piece. Determining age is not always easy. One guideline in pottery or ceramic pieces is crazing, a crackled look caused by the effect of changing temperature on pottery and glaze over a period of time. Wear is another. Teapots usually show the most wear, and the inside of a pot is harder to clean, and may become badly stained. If a teapot shows little or no wear, it may not have been used at all, may have been packed away, or have stood unused in a cupboard or on a shelf. But since few rooms remain at a constant temperature over the years, this is unlikely. Or it may be newer than you thought.

Dating English-made Pieces

English potteries produced the majority of the cottage ware from the 1920s to the early 1950s, with exceptions. Wade produced a few pieces of cottage ware in the 1930s as part of their Whimsey line; Sadler continues to produce a variety of teapots in the shape of stately homes or famous buildings; and Price Kensington makes a continuing line of cottage ware to the present day, using what appear to be the original blanks from the 1930s. Other potteries offer specialty pieces from time to time, notably teapots, canisters, cookie jars or biscuit barrels, and various household containers. Dating a piece is a way to determine value

Courtesy of Cordelia & Bob Mendoza

Repairs

Look for signs of wear, use, damage or repair. Examine the piece with a magnifying glass, especially around handles and lids which are the most common places for repairs. Some collectors who insist on pristine pieces go so far as to take along a small flashlight when they shop. When shown inside a piece, the light will reveal damage. Tap your finger on the piece. If you hear a *thunking* sound, rather than a clear ring, there may be an unseen crack or repair.

Some collectors don't mind well-repaired pieces if the price is right, especially if the piece is very old, particularly distinctive, or the only example you have been able to find to fill a collection. You may not mind a certain amount of damage if it's not too obvious or has been cleverly repaired. Some signs of wear are to be expected, and may give an indication of age. I've heard people call a chip under the lip of a cup or the bottom of a plate "no fault damage." Some feel this does not affect value, but many collectors disagree. This is a personal decision.

There are people who will carefully restore damaged pieces, for a price. This is painstaking, time-consuming, and expensive, depending on the extent of damage, but a carefully restored piece may keep its value, with no one the wiser.

For the most part, dealers try to be fair about prices, but they must take into consideration not only age, detail, condition, and maker, but also what they paid for the item, to ensure they will turn a profit, however small. Most dealers are business people, not hobbyists.

Values

The values given in this book are an average of those found for the same or similar pieces in shops, collections, and antique shows in various parts of the United States, British Columbia, and England. Prices on the west coast of the United States, in the mid-west and the east coast will vary according to the maker, rarity, and local popularity of an item. Royal Winton, Burlington, Beswick or other English makers that produced cottage ware over a limited time span are more expensive than those made in Japan or by Price Kensington, which continually produce the same pieces. Price Bros. or Kensington pieces are more rare because they were made before the two companies merged in 1934, so they bring more than Price & Kensington pieces. Occupied Japan commands a higher price than Japan, because the period of occupation was relatively short.

Read any reference books that include cottage/village ware in their listings for comparison, and remember, precise or not, prices are still a helpful guide to value. Prices in this book range from $5 to hundreds.

Introduction

The golden years of cottage ware were from the 1920s to the 1950s. English pieces are usually more detailed, hence more interesting, with many made in high relief. Cups, saucers, plates and bowls usually carry the image indicated by other shaped pieces in a set. Modern pieces are included as contrasting examples of what is produced today, and perhaps an indication for future collectibles.

There were many pieces made for useful household or table purposes, as opposed to solid, non-functional figurines. Many carry names like Country Villages, Friendly Village, and the like. It would be nearly impossible to find examples of each pottery that made cottage ware. Some, like advertising dog houses, may seem a bit out of the ordinary, but they are a type of humble abode that is a happy part of many households, and they have special smile appeal.

The word 'cottage' brings to mind a small, cozy, vine-covered English home nestled in an old-fashioned garden setting. Tea served from a cottage-shaped teapot brings a smile, even on the dreariest days. "Cozy" is what springs to mind when we see the highly collected household items shaped like cottages, pubs, houses, shops, other dwellings, and historic buildings. For the purpose of this book, I have given them the name "cottage ware" collectively.

Since the 1600s, Staffordshire, England, has been the heart and home of English pottery, because necessary materials for pottery making were close at hand: clay, coal, and water. The area was mentioned in the *Doomsday Book* (1086). Remnants of early Roman pottery have been found at Stoke-on-Trent. The word "stoke" comes from an old English word meaning "peace or holy place". Appropriately, a Saxon cross still stands in front of a church there, a modern reminder of days long gone.

The many potteries made the area famous for pottery making then, as now. The towns of Tunstall, Burslem, Hanley, Fenton, Longton, and Stoke were home to many potters competing to sell their wares. In 1910, these six towns combined to form the single town of Stoke-on-Trent. During the town's heyday in the late nineteenth century, when coal-fired kilns blackened the air, the town was called by some the ugliest in England. During World War II, it was said that the reason the enemy didn't bomb Stoke-on-Trent was because they thought someone had already done so before them. The townspeople joked that the air in Stoke-on-Trent "soots me well."

Illustration from *Sketches of Pottery Life and Character* by T. Hawley, A Staffordshire County Library Reprint.

The area was known as The Potteries because of the proliferation of pottery makers who toiled to supply local needs for plain earthenware pieces for everyday use, and special occasion pieces to recognize and celebrate Royal birthdays, coronations, and weddings. Burslem has been called Mother of Potteries because it was the birthplace and workshop of famous potters such as Josiah Wedgwood and Ralph Wood, creator of the Toby jug.

At some potteries today, it's possible to find pottery still being made by the old method of hand-forming the clay, firing it, decorating, and refiring the resultant pieces. Other than utilitarian table ware, everyday pottery included pastille burners, night lights, and spills. Many of them were imaginatively created to look like vine-covered cottages, castles, pubs, and other buildings and dwellings, simply decorated or with a profusion of flowers and even gilding.

A landmark for the English pottery industry was the introduction of tea to England in 1657. Its widespread use resulted in the gradual need for teapots and serving pieces. The teapot is probably the most widely produced of all pieces today, especially in Britain where tea is the leading beverage, with a reported 85 billion cups served daily.

Early Pieces

Night lights were hollow cottages with an opening in the back to place a candle or lighted wick in a small open container of whale or other oil placed inside the piece. There were cut out or lithophane windows to reflect the light. A lithophane is a porcelain panel with a raised or relief design. Light shining through the various thickness of the lithophane provided a subdued light. First made in Berlin in 1830, they were decoratively used in window plaques, lamp shades, and candle shields. In early days before electric lights, night lights or candles were necessary fixtures after dark.

A humorous story is told about another use for lithophanes, in the bottom of a teacup. The bottom of drinking mugs and teacups from Germany and Japan often have a lithophane of a woman, sometimes a nude. A story is told about a Japanese emperor who was planning to be wed. His wife, a jealous woman, demanded he give up his mistress. To please her, he agreed, but arranged for a special set of wedding porcelain to be made, with a lithophane with the image of his mistress's face in the bottom of one cup, the one he would drink from. Whenever he drank from the cup he would see her, unbeknownst to his wife. Some nightlights had roofs that lifted off for easier placement of the light.

Pastille burners held conical perfumed pills made of powdered willow wood charcoal, benzoin, perfumed oils, and gum arabic. They were burned in the days of perfunctory sanitation to keep rooms sweet-smelling and to mask unpleasant odors. Sometimes called perfume pots, they came in many forms: vine covered cottages or old world dwellings such as castles, churches, water mills, thatched farm cottages, Chinese pagodas, and pubs. Today, we have air fresheners in spray, solid form, or sachets, which serve the same function without the charm.

Spills were small vases to hold straws, rolled papers, or small twigs used as fire lighters for the family fireplace, a necessary part of every home, to heat the home.

Crime Cottages were an early form of cottage in the 19th century, so-called because they were models of notorious British houses that had been the scene of a famous murder. They were created to satisfy the public's fascination with gruesome events. (Not so very different from today's society.) A popular example includes Red Barn, Polstead (1828), the scene of the murder of Maria Masten by William Corder. Another example, even more famous, was Potash Farm, the home of a Cornish man, James Rush, who murdered his neighbor, Mr. Jeremy. The finest of these cottage images were made by the potters Sampson Smith of Longdon, and William Kent of Burslem. It is still possible to find a night light in the form of a crime cottage.

Later Pieces

Little by little, other useful items were made as cottage ware: jugs, biscuit barrels, condiment sets, mugs, and many other everyday pieces. When the cottage ware production exploded in the 1930s, whole sets were created in cottage form, especially breakfast dishes to add a cheery note to a cold winter morning. Eggcups, teapots, jam pots, toast racks, covered butter and cheese dishes, and more were made then. A great many examples have survived the years, despite daily use. Today they are highly collectible.

Some cottage ware is known by old English names, like Olde Water Mill, and Olde English Cottage, and some were made to represent a famous cottage, such as Anne Hathaway's Cottage. Royal Winton made examples of this.

It was but a small step from early, old-world pieces to the more modern architectural pieces. Most of the early cottage ware has come from England, especially Staffordshire, but over the years cottage ware has come from many parts of the world, including England, China, Japan, the Philippines, Occupied Japan, the United States, and Western Germany. Pieces from Occupied Japan (1948-1952) and Western Germany (1945-1990) can easily be dated, others take a bit of research. But that is part of the fun.

English potters Price Bros and Kensington were known for cottage ware from the 1920s. Today, Price-Kensington still produces a line of cottage ware resembling Price Bros.' early pieces. Sadler is another English producer of pottery noted for its teapots, many of which are in the style of famous stately homes. Some other English potteries are Beswick, Burlington, Coalport, Copeland, Crown Devon, Devon, Derby, Hanley, Keele Street Pottery, Royal Winton, Shorter & Sons, Wade, Worcester, Arthur Wood. Examples of most of these can be found on the antiques market. They sometimes use similar color themes and designs, but each has its own distinctive look, readily recognized by a discerning collector

The photographs show a sampling of pieces, some whimsical, some practical, all imaginative, decorative, and useful in function. The common thread is the *use* of a piece. They were designed to bring a smile on the dreariest of days.

Replica of a pot bank. Early potteries were housed in what were called "pot banks," with everything close at hand and under one roof, from clay to kiln to living quarters. *Courtesy of Reg Bladen.*

What The Potteries Produced

The novel idea of producing ordinary table and kitchen ware in the form of cottages and village shops proved very popular. As in real-life towns and villages, there is a tremendous variety of color, style, and architecture in the ware, making them an appealing collectible.

At first glance, many of these imaginative pieces may appear to be alike but, like houses, cottages, and shops in the same village or neighborhood, there are differences in architectural details, colors, sizes, and shapes. Colors range from dark to light, bright to white, and structures have the appearance of brick, stone, stucco, or half-timbered wood. Some are as simple as a child's line drawing, others elaborately and carefully detailed, and only limited by the artist's or potter's imagination. Many have a fairytale appearance and appeal. Frequently, the purpose of a piece is painted on — a tea canister or caddy may be labeled as a teahouse; a flour canister, a bakery; a sugar canister, an ice cream shop; or a coffee container, a cafe.

Potteries produced a series of household ware that might be varied the next year, or, if it proved unpopular, be eliminated from future production. Each pottery had its own variation of size, color, roof line, and placement of windows or doors. Color differences came about because more than one artist applied his or her brush. Potteries, many of which were short-lived, made similar pieces because they 'borrowed' ideas from each other. Most, but not all, are hand-painted under the final glaze; others are cold-painted, with hand-painting as the finishing touch. Be careful if you buy a cold-painted piece. Frequently, a dealer will tape a teapot lid to protect it from breakage. This may result in the paint coming off with the tape, devaluing the piece.

Here are some of the variations to look for:

Design: One, two, or three story

Shape: Square, round, rectangular, oval, or conical.

Windows: Single-or multi-paned; square, round, rectangular, or dormer.

Doorways: Covered or flat; vine or flower-covered, with or without a porch.

Roofs: Flat, peaked, tiled, thatched, or gabled.

Subjects: Cottages are probably the most popular, followed by pubs and shops.

Size: Examples pictured vary widely in size. The largest, a cookie jar, is about 24" tall, the smallest, a mustard pot, 1 1/2" high. Large pieces, such as kitchen jugs, canister sets, and biscuit or cookie jars, are still produced, but the older pieces and special edition pieces are the most collectible.

What pieces might we expect to find?

Pitchers, jugs, creamers; tumblers, cups and saucers, mugs, banks, vases, square sugars (for cubes); round sugars — some with lids; bowls and plates; egg cups — footed or un-footed and with or without trays; household jars; condiment sets and shakers — with or without trays. Small salt and pepper shakers were for table use while large salt and pepper shakers were for use at the stove. Covered butter and cheese dishes, creamers and sugars... the list is seemingly endless. All can be found as cottage pieces, in high and bas relief, or with building details only indicated by painting or transfer design.

Some potteries made toothpick holders, which today have many collectors. They were commonly used as part of a table setting and also were made from glass, until about 1900, when the upper classes decided cleaning one's teeth at the table was not a dignified part of elegant dining; then some toothpick holders were banished to the china cabinet. However, many remained on the table in the majority of homes and can be found today.

Ashtrays were also once an expected part of most households. Less common today, they are collectible in their own right. Most popular from the 1920s to 1960s, when tobacco advertisements were commonplace and movie actors and actresses were usually smoking. The public copied their behavior. Smoking was an accepted social behavior and ashtrays were provided for guests, whether or not the host or hostess indulged in the habit. Today, fewer smoking-related items are made, and 'tobacciana' pieces are a sought-after collectibles.

We may assume a piece with an opening is a planter or flower holder, no matter how small, but the original use may have been as a pincushion, toothpick holder, or match holder. Match holders can usually be identified because they had a roughened area for striking a match. What is thought to be a bank might in fact have been intended as a receptacle for used razor blades, after the advent of single blades, and before the invention of electric razors.

The Cottage Ware

ADVERTISING

What better way to advertise a company name than by putting it on a piece of pottery used every day in the kitchen or on the breakfast table? An eye-catching, brightly colored cookie jar is an example of making advertising pay off in a much more subtle way than a newspaper ad or radio/television commercial. If every time a child reaches for a cookie or a dog biscuit for Fido he sees a doghouse with the pet food name on it, which brand do you think he'll want Mom to bring home?

Other gimmicks include free giveaways for buying a product or opening a new account. A bank may give away penny banks to attract new juvenile accounts and future investors. What fun for a child to save his/her pennies in a Snoopy bank in the form of a doghouse. He may not remember the bank's name, but his parents will, and the memory will always remain with the child. When he starts a bank account as an adult, he will remember the bank of his childhood memories.

Liquor producers such as Jim Beam and others have for years found it effective to offer their product in collectible containers. The piece itself carries the message; the maker is unimportant. Advertising pieces usually have a theme, and are commissioned to commemorate or celebrate a memorable event or date, to sell a product, or to attract tourist trade to an area.

1. **Nestle's Chocolate Co.** (USA) Cookie Jar, 9 1/2" high, in the form of a welcoming white house with bright red trim and yellow tile roof, sure to brighten any kitchen. It was handy to keep Toll House cookies, and an ever-present reminder of the product. There is a Nestle sign in front, lest you forget the name. Since Toll House (chocolate chip) cookies were first introduced in the 1940s, they have been a universally popular snack. This may have been a send-away-for promotional piece (box tops or labels). Encised mark: Limited Edition Nestle, Toll House, Cookie Jar 1992. £40. $95

2. **Walter Kendall Fiver** (USA) Cookie or dog biscuit jar. 8" high. Walter Kendall is known as a producer of dog food. Their doghouse is white with a bright red roof. No manufacturer's backstamp. Especially appealing to a child. £25. $39

3. **Bank of America** Penny bank in form of a dog house with red roof. 7" high. The highly popular cartoon character, Snoopy, is asleep on top. Possibly given as a premium for opening a new bank account. Mark: Bank of America. World Rights Reserved. £10. $25

Bank of America penny bank base marking

4. **Pennsylvania Tourist's Souvenir**. 4" high penny bank in the shape of a dark brown cabin. No maker's mark, but the top is marked Penna Dutchland. £10. $15

5. **Log Cabin Syrup** Syrup jug. 7" high, in the form of a log cabin. The state of Vermont is famous for its maple trees and its product, maple syrup, for many years produced by the Log Cabin Syrup Co. Made by Unity Stoneware Co., Newport, Vermont. The chimney is the pouring spout. £12. $20

UNITY STONEWARE CO.
BOX 685
NEWPORT, VT 05855

Log Cabin Syrup jug base marking

7. **Vinicola-Baciaccio Italy**. Liquor Bottle/Decanter, 8" high. Grey edifice, representing Paris, France's Arc de Triomph. Probably commissioned in France and made in Italy as a commemorative piece for tourists to France. In raised letters on bottom: Vinicola-Baciaccio, Italy-Florence, Produced 1968 £15. $19

6. **Old Taylor Distillery Company**. Liquor Bottle/Decanter, 8 3/4" high. Replica of Old Taylor's company building, with sign, The Old Taylor Distillery Company across the front. Probably an anniversary promotional piece. Grey block building. £20. $30

OLD TAYLOR
KENTUCKY STRAIGHT BOURBON WHISKEY
DISTILLED & BOTTLED BY
THE OLD TAYLOR DISTILLERY COMPANY
FRANKFORT, KY. LOUISVILLE, KY.
DISTRIBUTED BY NATIONAL DISTILLERS PRODUCTS CO.

KENTUCKY STRAIGHT BOURBON WHISKEY
86 PROOF ONE QUART
THIS WHISKEY IS FOUR YEARS OLD

Old Taylor decanter base marking

8. **Ezra Brooks Distillery** Liquor Bottle/Decanter, 7 3/4" high. Low building with 24K gold-roofed additions. Sticker imprinted with "24K Gold" raised mark: Heritage China, Ezra Brooks, 1970 Club. £20. $35

9. **Ezra Brooks Distillery** Liquor Bottle/Decanter, 9 1/2" high. Low, round, blue building with a shiny gold plane on top. Commemorative piece. Mark on bottom: "Wichita Centennial" £20. $35

10. **Jim Beam Distillery. Heritage China, 1970 Club** Liquor Bottle/Decanter, 7 1/2" high. Replica of ranch house. Sign on front: "Ponderosa Ranch, Nevada." "On Lake Tahoe" is printed on back. Collector's piece. Raised mark on bottom: Creation of James B. Beam Distillery Co., NY-DRB-230, Genuine Regal China. Miller 1969 145. £15. $25

10a. **Mrs. Field's Cookies** appeared on the U.S. market in the 1980s and have occasionally offered advertising pieces, such as this cookie jar, to the public. This cookie shop is 7 3/4" tall to the peak of the roof, 7 1/4" wide across the front of the brown roof, and 4 1/3" deep. There is an eye-catching red striped awning over the window and, over the door, a red curved awning with "Mrs. Fields" written in white. An aproned figure is shown in relief inside the shop window, and through the window in the door one sees a relief table, chairs, and menu. Marked "Made in China" on the bottom. £20.

ARTONE (England)

Artone appears to have been a small pottery that operated for a short period of time. After two years of searching, I was only able to find one small mustard pot with their name, but was told there were others.

Artone base marking

11. **Artone** Mustard Pot, 1 1/2" high. Tiny half-timbered two-story building. "The Olde Curiosity Shop". This is the smallest piece found. It may be just a one-off, or part of a mini-condiment set. £32. $45

12. **Avon** Canister, 8 1/2" high. Blue roof, double doors. £30. $55

AVON COSMETIC COMPANY (United States)

Avon has been called America's most successful cosmetic company, known since 1898 by their slogan, "Avon Calling". Their products are sold internationally by representatives who are rewarded for their productivity, as shown by volume of sales.

Years ago, I was an Avon representative, and still remember how exciting it was when my Christmas sales were high enough to earn the "walking dolls" my daughters longed for.

Canisters pictured are part of Townhouse Canister Collection produced in the 1980s. All are stamped "Hand Painted in Brazil Exclusively for Avon Representatives" high These neat, pretty, two-story tile-roofed houses are a limited collectible, not listed under "Advertising" highsince they were not made for sale to the public. They have an Avon welcome mat at the front door. One has a basket in relief on the mat, another a relief figure of an Avon Lady waiting at the front door. Avon also featured a 1982 Christmas canister, "McConnell's General Store. There may be other special issues as well.

Avon Townhouse Canister Collection base marking

Avon General Store base marking

13. **Avon** Canister, 8 1/2". Two-story townhouse, white, blue roof. Double doors. "Welcome Avon" on doormat £30. $55

14. **Avon** Canister, 11 1/2" high. Three-story townhouse, with Avon lady standing on front stoop. "Welcome Avon" on doormat. Sirgle door. £60. $95

15. **Avon** Canister, 9 1/2" high. Two-story, with blue covered basket in relief on the "Welcome Avon" doormat. £35. $59

16. **Avon** Canister, 7" high. Two-story townhouse, white, tan roof. Single door. £27. $40

17. **Avon** Canister, 7" high. Two-story townhouse, white, tan roof. Single door. £27. $40

BESWICK (Staffordshire, England)

Beswick (pronounced *bez'ik*) was begun at Longton, Staffordshire in the 1890s by James Wright Beswick and his son John. A grandson, also John, took over operation in 1936. They are still in operation today, part of Doulton since 1973. They are known for their figures, especially animals of all sorts. Beswick cottage ware with Beswick farm animals is an especially appealing way to display a collection.

Beswick's cottage ware was produced in the 1930s, and is mostly round in shape, with thatched roofs and cris-cross window panes. An exception is a covered butter dish depicted as an early American-style log cabin.

Beswick Ware base marking, used from 1936.

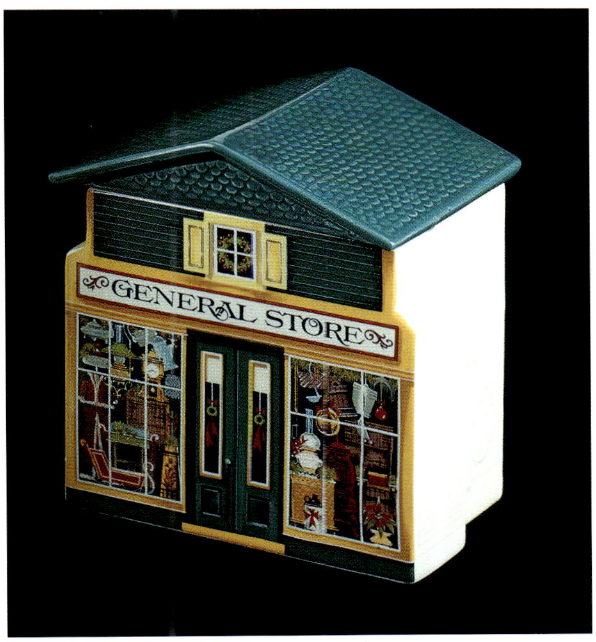

18. **Avon** Canister, 5 3/4" high. Sign, "The General Store." Dark green roof and front of attic windows. Only the front of this piece has shop design; other sides are plain cream-colored. Christmas piece available to the public. Stamped on bottom: McConnell's Corners General Store, Christmas 1982. $33. £45

19. **Beswick** Covered Cheese on tray. Square, 5 1/2" high. £55. $85

20. **Beswick** Covered Cheese on tray. Square 5" high. Unusual in that it is in the image of a log cabin, which is thought of as American. £45. $75

21. **Beswick** Covered Cheese or butter box. 4 1/2" high. Round, with tray attatched to cottage and lid that lifts off. Unusual. £50. $110

22. **Beswick** Cheese Cover. Round, on plate. 4 1/2" high. £40. $90

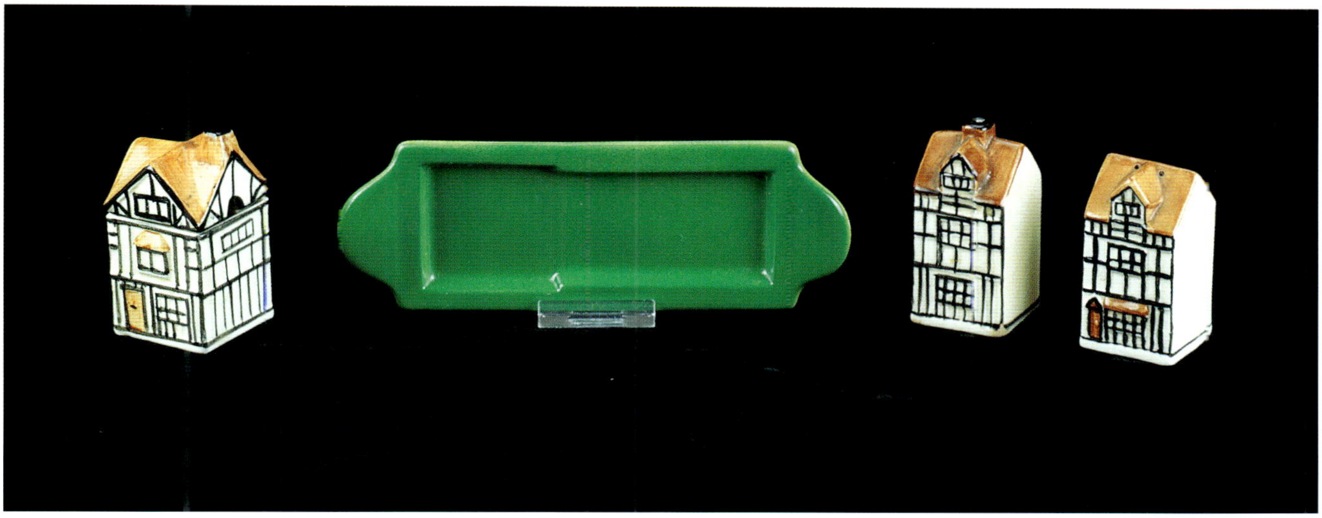

23. **Beswick** Condiment Set on green rectangular tray, 3 1/4" high. Three half-timbered Tudor houses. Mustard (left), Salt, Pepper. $50. £110

24. **Beswick** Biscuit Barrel/Box, unhandled, 6 1/2" high. Different in that a door is shown on each side. £60. $135

25. **Beswick** Jug, 5" high. £40. $95

26. **Beswick** Coffee Pot, 7"high. £55. $110

27. **Beswick** Teapot, Round Roof, 6" high. Blue Windows. £60. $110

28. **Beswick** Sugar, Round, Open, 2 3/4" high. Gnarled handles. £25. $39

29. **Beswick** Creamer, Round, 2 3/4" high, Gnarled handle. £25. $39

30. **Beswick** Sugar, Round, Gnarled Handles, open. 2 3/4" high. £25. $39

BLOCK (USA)

Block is a modern American company that produced some interesting examples of village ware. The example pictured is a tan, two-story country home cookie jar with salt and pepper shakers to match. We were unable to find other pieces. There is an attic window in the side of the dark green roof, and much shrubbery. Labled "Country Village," it was made in China.

Block base marking

31. **Block** Canister, 10" high. £35. $55

32. **Block** Salt and Pepper, 2 3/4" square. Pepper (left) represents a barn with one chimney and three pouring holes in top. Salt, depicting a house, has two chimneys and only two pouring holes on top. £20. $35

BURLINGTON (England)

Burlington ware was produced by John Shaw & Sons Ltd, in Longton. Part of Staffordshire Potteries, in operation from 1931 - 1963, The Burlington mark was used from 1959-1963. Their cottages were mostly conical in shape, half-timbered, with golden brown thatched roofs. Doors are usually dark brown; windows are shades of blue and grey. Back stamps vary only in size, depending on the size of a piece.

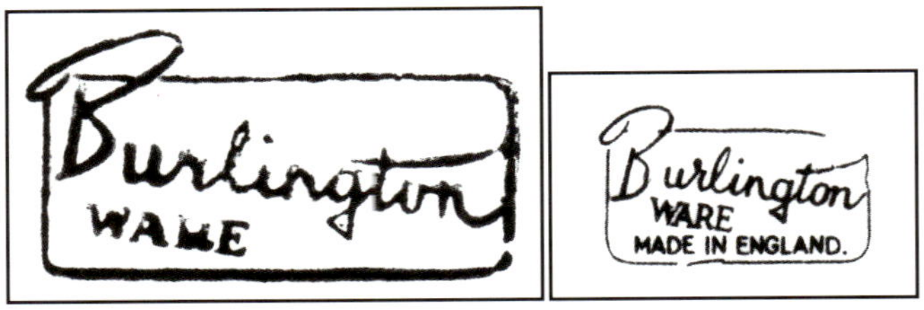

Burlington Ware base markings

34. **Burlington** Teapot with different look from other Burlington pieces. Square, 7 1/2" high. £35. $65.

33. **Burlington** Butter, Covered, on oval dish. 5 1/2" high on 6" long tray. £49. $125

35. **Burlington** Teapot, 6" high. £40. $85.

BURLINGTON WARE / DEVON COBB
(England)

This is a variation of Burlington, possibly in operation during the same years. The cottage pieces with the Devon Cobb backstamp are much the same as those marked simply Burlington. Design and coloring are nearly identical. Most have the printed Burlington mark, with Devon Cobb also incised on each piece.

36. **Burlington** Butter, Covered, on oval dish. 4" high. £40. $85.

38. **Burlington Ware / Devon Cobb** Coffee Pot, 6 3/4" high. £50. $105.

37. **Burlington** Covered Sugar, with handles. Oval, 3 3/4" high. £30. 39.

39. **Burlington Ware / Devon Cobb** Teapot, 6" high. £55. 110.

40. **Burlington Ware / Devon Cobb** Coffee Pot, 7 1/2" high. £55. $95.

41. **Burlington Ware / Devon Cobb** Covered Sugar, 3 1/2" high. £25. $39.

42. **Burlington Ware / Devon Cobb** Teapot, 6 1/2" high. £50. $105.

43. **Burlington Ware / Devon Cobb** Creamer, 3" high. £20. $30.

44. **Burlington Ware / Devon Cobb** Jam/Marmalade Pot, Covered, 4 1/2" high, opening for spoon £39. $65.

46. **Burlington Ware / Devon Cobb** Covered Sugar, 3 1/2" high. £25. $39.

45. **Burlington Ware / Devon Cobb** Milk Jug, 4" high. £25. $35.

47. **Burlington Ware / Devon Cobb** Creamer, 3" high. £20. $30.

CADCOURT (England)

Information on Cadcourt is unknown. Since pieces are also difficult to find (even in England), it must have been a small, short-lived pottery studio.

CHINA

China has long made, and continues to make and export, cottage ware to various parts of the world with the backstamp of 'China'. Also, because of cheaper labor costs, many U.S. companies have commissioned potteries in China to produce their order with the U.S. company name. U.S. import laws require the country of origin to be marked on the item. Examples: Block (USA), Fitz & Floyd (USA) and Sadler (England). Fitz & Floyd sells giftware internationally through catalogs, with showrooms in major U.S. cities, but it does not manufacture what they sell. Several other examples of modern ware are pictured, mostly cookie jars and canisters.

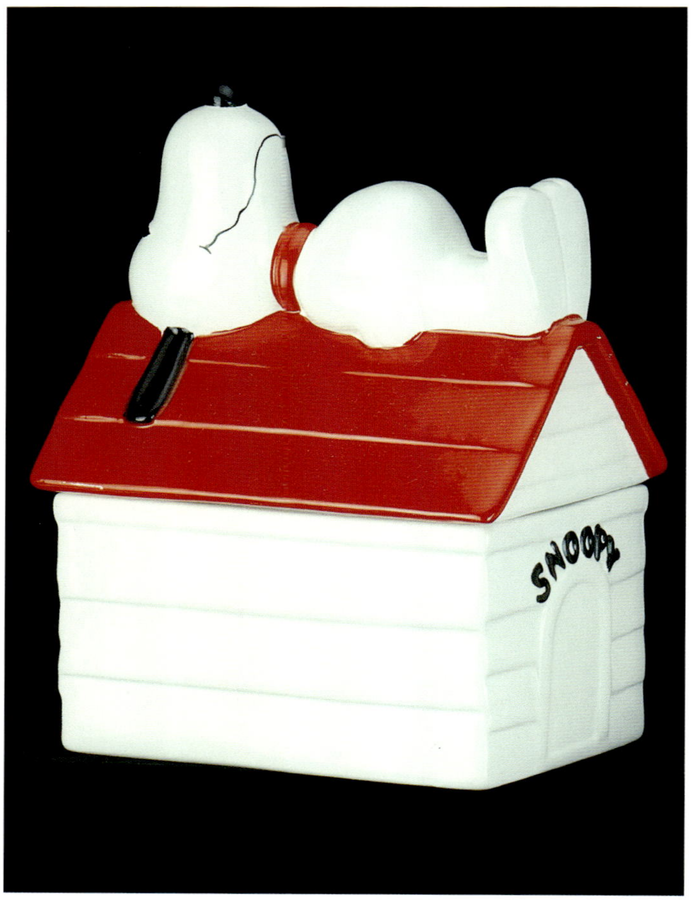

48. **China** Cookie or Dog Biscuit Jar, 10 1/2" high. In shape of cartoon figure, Snoopy, asleep on top of his dog house. White, red roof. $65.

49. **China** Cookie Jar, 9" high. "Main Street Theatre." Fitz and Floyd (distributors). $55.

50. **Cadcourt** Butter Top (plate missing). 4 1/2" high. Half-timbered cottage, thatched roof. £20. $30.

51. **China** Teapot, pastel, 6 1/2" high. Multi-paned, blue windows. Identifying sticker. Mark on bottom would seem to indicate it was made for export to France. We found it in England, where it may have been taken as a souvenir in the luggage of a British tourist. Mark: Made in China, Fabrique en Chine. £20. $35.

53. **China** Teapot, 5 1/2" high. Apricot colored teahouse, green pagoda-shaped roof. £15. $25.

52. **China** Salt and Pepper. Piggy-backed to lock like a single cottage piece. 3" high. Marked "Made in China." £8. $15.

54. **China** Teapot, 5 1/2" high. Apricot colored teahouse, green pagoda-shaped roof. Identical to #53 with slight variation of color. £15. $25.

CROWN DEVON (England)

Crown Devon is the trade name of S. Fielding and Co. Ltd, an English firm founded after toward the end of the 18th Century. They were part of Staffordshire Potteries, with production that included earthenware household and kitchen pieces and majolica. Known as Crown Devon after 1911, and after 1917 as Crown Devon & Fielding. In 1930 Fielding was dropped, which dates their cottage ware to the 1930s. Included are numbers indicating month and year of production dates. The pieces pictured all have orange roofs and appear to be part of the same series.

Crown Devon
base marking

56. **China** Town Hall, 7 1/2" high

55, 56, and 57. **China** Canisters, special Christmas set. White, elegant gold trim, white village pieces. Marked, "Home for the Holidays, Christmas Set." £60. $95 set.

55. **China** Village Church, 10 1/2" high

57. **China** Town Building, 6" high

58. **Crown Devon** Jam Pot, Covered, lots of greenery. 4" high. Cottage pub, "Berry Inn". £45. $95.

59. **Crown Devon** Condiment Set, 3-piece, rectangular, 3 3/4" high. £50. $110.

60. **Crown Devon** Condiment Set, 3-piece on round green tray, 2 3/4" high. House, "Salt Box". Covered Jam Pot in the form of a windmill. £50. $115.

T. DEAN AND SONS (England)

Tunstall, Staffordshire. Possibly Thomas Dean & Sons, Tunstall, although the mark on this teapot is different from those found in reference books. Operated from 1789 - 1947, producing earthenware. Part of Staffordshire Potteries.

T. Dean & Sons
base marking

61. **T. Dean & Sons**. Teapot, Square, cornered handle and spout, 6 1/2". Double brown chimneys. £45. $75.

DELFT

Potteries in the town of Delft, Holland, produced pottery of this sharply colored blue and white in the 15th century and before. Few remain, altough the style and color are widely copied. Today, "Delft" is a word used to describe the particular shade of blue that the Dutch potteries are noted for.

Most of the pictured pieces are part of the same canister set, all in the same vivid blue and white colors. Marked "Handpainted Delft Blue DAIC." My research did not turn up any information about the DAIC mark. Probably a distributor.

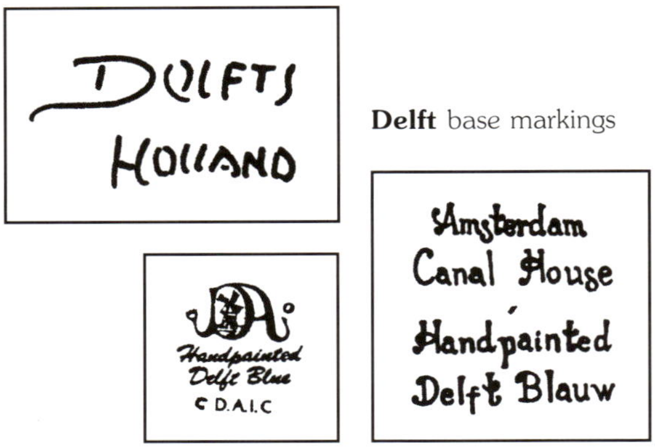

Delft base markings

63. **Delft** Canister, 9" high. Marked DAIC. £15. $30.

62. **Delft** Canister, 7" high. Marked DAIC. £12. $25.

64. **Delft** Canister, 8" high. Marked DAIC. £20. $29.

65. **Delft** Canister, 7" high. Marked DAIC. £19. $25.

67. **Delft** Teapot, 8" high. Lid is on right side of rcof. Marked DAIC. £20. $30.

66. **Delft** Ashtray, 3 1/2" high with cigarette rest and open chimney for smoke. Hand-printed. Delft Holland. £12. $19.

68. **Delft** Jam Pot, 4 1/2" high, with lid. Marked DAIC. £12. $20.

70. **Delft** Canister/Container, 4 1/2" high. Marked DAIC. £10. $15.

69. **Delft** Vase or Kitchen Utensil Holder, 5 1/4" high. Impressed mark on bottom, "Holland Floral 03 Patented." £13. $20.

71. **Delft** Canister/Container, 4 3/4" high. Marked DAIC. £10. $15.

DEVON (England)

Devon, especially South Devon and the little town of Torquay, is a popular seaside resort area and vacation spot. Since the late 19th Century, a number of Devon potteries produced novelty pottery pieces of various kinds as tourist momentos. Pottery was an appropriate industry because both white and natural red clay were plentiful. Devon pottery has a distinctive look, with heavy slip and low (bas) relief.

Red clay was used to make terra cotta folk pottery, known as 'motto ware' and 'scrafitti' because of the various mottos, sayings, and proverbs scratched into the heavy slip and into the red clay. Much of this was done by children employed by the pottery, resulting in mispelled words, which added a certain amount of charm. Cottages were a popular subject, usually by illustration, not by shape of the piece.

73. **Devon** Open Sugar or Jam Pot, 3 1/2" high. Square, vine covered cottage. Marked "Torquay Pottery." £22. $39.

72. **Devon** Creamer, white slip, brown inside, 2 3/4" high. Square, vine-covered cottage. £18. $25.

74. **Devon** Spill, 3 3/4" high. Cottage, water mill on back. Peaked thatched roof. White, bright colors in relief. £23. $45.

75. **Devon** Jug, relief ware, 5" high. Marked "Bovey Art Pottery, Devon." £20. $45.

EMPIRE PORCELAIN CO LTD (England)

Empire Porcelain Co operated in Stoke, Staffordshire, from 1896. They produced earthenware, including cottage ware, which was made in the 1930s. Their pieces represented half-timbered houses—white, with brown and yellow roofs and blooming flowers in profusion around the house and twining over the door.

Empire Ware base marking

76. **Devon** Covered Sugar, 3 1/2" high. White slip, "Made in Devon." £20. $29.

77. **Empire Porcelain Co.** Jam Pot, covered, 3 3/4" high. Half-timbered house. £25. $45.

78. **Empire Porcelain Co.** Jam Pot, covered, 3 3/4" high. Half-timbered house. £25. $45.

ENGLAND

We found a number of examples of English cottages with only an encised mark, England, and no indication of the maker. Some were recognizable because of color and design, but others had no identification mark, but may once have had a paper or foil sticker. A set of household jars fell into this category. Luckily, the dealer who offered it as a set remembered similar pieces as give-away prizes at country fairs or fetes in the 1950s, in much the same way carnival glass was given out at American carnivals and country fairs.

80, 81, 82. Fair prizes. These canisters are all alike and unmarked except for the purpose: (Coffee, Tea, Sugar.)

79. **Empire Porcelain Co.** Jug, 4 1/2" high. White, with brown and yellow roof. Shrubs and flowers around the house, vines growing over the door. Some four-paned windows, others blank with dark brown outlines. £30. $50.

80. **England** Canister, "Coffee." 6" high. Cream-colored, brown half-timbered markings, greenery, and dark gray thatched roof. £18. $29.

81. **England** Canister, "Tea". 6" high. Cream-colored, half-timbered markings, greenery, and dark gray thatched roof. £18. $29.

83. **England** Covered Butter, 6 1/2" high. Art Deco Chrome Tray with glass liner. Butter-colored cottage, thatched roof. Orange-red chimney and tile on lean-to. Half-timbered. £60. $110.

82. **England** Canister, "Sugar". 6" high. Cream-colored, half-timbered markings, greenery, and dark gray thatched roof. £18. $29.

84. **England** Butter Box, thatched roof, 4 1/4" high. Tan vine-covered cottage. Dark brown chimney. £30. $65.

85. **England** Teapot, round pub "The Dog and Duck", 4 3/4" high. Cream colored, brown handle. Two separated entry doors. £45. $80.

87. **England** Teapot, ivory colored, 5 1/2" high. Orange floral accents, chimney and handle. Many-paned windows. £30. $60.

86. **England** Teapot, square cottage, 5 1/4" high. Tan thatch with greenery. Brown handle. £35. $65.

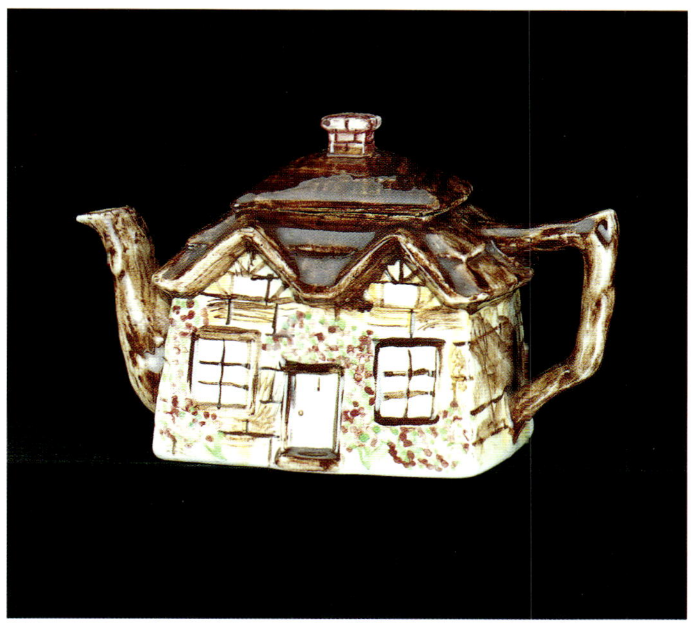

88. **England** Teapot, cream and brown, brown roof, 5 1/2" high. £30. $60.

89. **England** Covered Butter, green-edged tray, 5" high, tray 7 1/2" long. Ivory-colored with orange-brown thatch and chimney. £40. $60.

90. **England** Shaker, 4 1/2" high. Tall, reddish, with orange tiled roof. £30. $55.

91. **England** Shaker, 3 3/4" high. Two-story, medium brown, black roof. £30. $55.

92. **England** Pastille Burner, 4" high. Black-roofed two-story gray brick house. "Marley" sign above the door. Circa early 1900s Opening for fire source has obvious signs of much use. £25. $40.

DEREK FOWLER STUDIO (England)

This is a modern piece made by one of the many pottery studios operating in Staffordshire over the years.

93. **Derek Fowler Studio** Night Light, 5 1/2" high. Pub "The Barley Mow." Open windows to allow the inside light to be seen. Brick building, brown thatched roof. Wired for British wiring. No plug. It has long been the custom in England where there are a variety of electrical outlet choices, to allow for choice of plug needed for outlet in buyer's home. £25. $40.

JAPAN

Japan has long been a prolific exporter of pottery and porcelain, especially to the American market. Any piece marked "Japan" was made after 1920 and World War I, when the U.S. passed laws requiring the country of origin be printed in English. Before that, Japanese pieces were marked "Nippon," Japanese for "Japan."

First efforts to protect United States products from imported goods were made with the 1890s McKinley Act, requiring imported goods to carry the name of the country of origin. Around 1914, "Made in" was also required. Remembering these dates is helpful in dating any piece.

After World War II, until 1952, Allied Forces occupied Japan. During these few years, most of Japan's ware was marked "Made in Occupied Japan" (See section on Occupied Japan). "Foreign" was another mark that may have begun during the occupation years to avoid using the word "Japan," which was not popular in England and the U.S. directly after WW II. Examples of Japanese-made pieces are plentiful.

Instead of looking for a variety of makers, this study looked for variation of cottage pieces. Many are nearly identical to English pieces. Pieces pictured in this category are variously marked "Japan," "Made in Japan," and "Foreign."

Made in Japan, Marutomo Ware base marking

Enesco importer's base marking

94. **Japan** Condiment set, 3" high on 7" long green tray. Colorful pagoda design in red, yellow, and blue. Marked "Foreign." £20. $35.

95. **Japan** Jam Pot, 3 1/2" high. Yellow, square tiled roof cottage. Green roof. Relief figures in doorway. Marked "Foreign." £13. $30.

96, 97, and 98 appear to be part of a matched set or series. We bought each one in a different country—one in Vancouver, British Columbia, one in England, and one in Northern California.

96. **Japan** Little Teapot, 4". Cream colored, thatched roof, round cottage. Bees on front of cottage and on roof. Circle mark on bottom, "Made in Japan." £20. $35.

97. **Japan** Salt and Pepper Shakers on green tray with finger hole for carrying. Bees on cream-colored cottage. Round roofs. Oval, shaped, 4" long tray. No mark. £15. $25.

98. **Japan** Jug. Cream-colored round cottage with greenery and bees, 2 ½" high. No mark. £20. $30.

99. **Japan** Teapot, Musical, 7" high. Plays a lilting tune. Two-story white brick townhouse, dark brown roof. Sticker on bottom reads, "Hand Crafted, Otagiri Japan". Washing instructions printed on sticker on handle. Otagiri is a Japanese exporter. £20. $39.

100. **Japan** Shaker, tan and cream colored, 4" high. Low relief, thatched roof. Identical to #102. Marked "Made in Japan." £15. $25.

101. **Japan** Butter Box, Covered, 4" high. Tan and cream colored, thatched roof, low relief. Marked "Made in Japan." £20. $40.

102. **Japan** Shaker, tan and cream colored, 4" high. Thatched roof, low relief. Identical to #100, although both have 7 holes. Salt shakers usually have fewer holes. £15. $25.

103. **Japan** Teapot, 5" high, brown and cream colored. Square, thatched roof cottage. Windows and doors outlined in dark brown. Marked "Made in Japan." £18. $30.

105, and 106. **Japan** Sugar, 2 3/4" high, and Cream, 3" high Set. Matches teapot, #104. Round cottage, green roof. "Made in Japan." £15. $25 set.

104. **Japan** Teapot, 5 1/2" high. Round cottage, green roof, brown handle and spout. Marked "Made in Japan." £19. $28.

107. **Japan** Covered Jam Pot, 3 1/2" high. Pub, brown roof, relief figures at door. Sign on door, "Ye Olde Curiosity Shop". Same blank as #95, but different coloring and mark. Marked "Marutomo Ware" with "T" in a circle, and "Made in Japan." £20. $30.

108. **Japan** Creamer, 3" high. Cream colored, with green and brown. "Made in Japan." £15. $23.

109. **Japan** Teapot, 5" high, cream colored, brown and green accents. Hand-printed mark, "Made in Japan." £20. $30.

110, and 111. **Japan** Sugar, 3 1/2" high, Creamer, 3" high. Set matches #109. £22. $35 set.

112. **Japan** Open Sugar, square, 2" high. Cream colored cottage, blue door. Faded mark , "Made in Japan" below a horseshoe shaped wreath with "Pico." £18. $25.

113. **Japan** Creamer, 2 1/4" high. Cream colored, brown accents. Square, handle and spout on corners. Dark blue door, black outline on windows. Same "Pico" mark as #112. £17. $23.

114. **Japan** Teapot, 4 1/2" high. Square. Creamy yellow, brown handle, spout, and outlines. £20. $30.

115. **Japan** Salt/Pepper, 2 3/4" high, on 6 1/2" long green tray. Cream colored with greenery and near-black accents. £22. $35.

116. **Japan** Cookie Jar, 9" high to top of handle. "Cookie House" in black on front. Square, plastic-wrapped reed handle. Pink, green, brown. "Made in Japan." £25. $45.

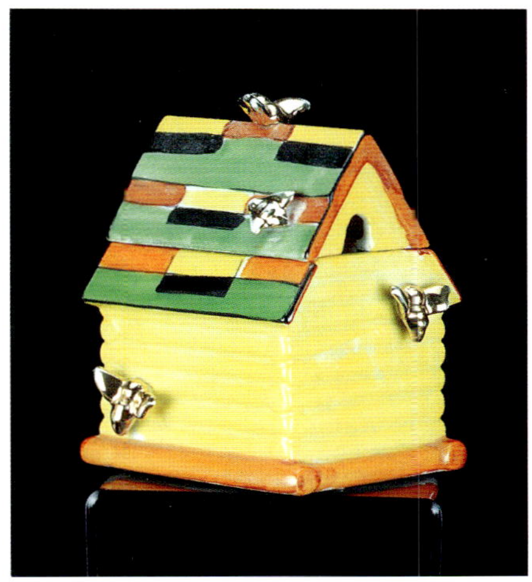

117. **Japan** Honey Pot, 4" high. Art Deco style. Yellow, green, black, orange, gold bees. Spoon opening in lid. £23. $39.

118. **Japan** Teapot, 4" high. Ivory, with light blue tile roof. Round, pink door, greenery. Impressed mark, "Japan." £19. $25.

119. **Japan** Covered Sugar, 3 3/4" high. Brown thatched ivory colored brick cottage. Blue chimney. Marked "Japan." £19. $25.

120. **Japan** Teapot, 5 3/4" high. Square, ivory colored, golden brown tiled roof, greenery, pink flowers. Marked "Made in Japan" with SS within a diamond shaped outline. £22. $35.

121. **Japan** Jam Jar, 3 1/2" high. (Matches 120). Ivory colored , golden brown tiled roof, greenery, pink flowers. Circle mark, "Maurutomo Ware. Made in Japan" "T" in center of circle. £22. $35.

122 and 123. **Japan** Set. Creamer, 3" high, Covered Sugar, 4 1/2" high. Square. Creamer has cornered handle, no handles on sugar. Cottage, yellow thatch, orange chimney, greenery. £18. $25 set.

124. **Japan** Condiment Set. Salt, Pepper, Mustard/Jam. Salt shaker is a tiny building, Pepper shaker is water mill, Jam Pot is attached to stand. Stand is a green hill. Unusual design. Shakers 4" high, Stand 5 1/4" in length. "Made in Japan." £60. $75.

125. **Japan** Match Holder, 3 1/2" high. Bird sitting on bird house. Blue windows, quarter moon on side. "Made in Japan." £9. $15.

126. **Japan** Egg Cup, 1 1/2" high. Pale paste. Mark too worn to read. £1. $5.

127 and 128. **Japan** Set. Covered Sugar, 4" high, half-covered Creamer, 3 3/4" high. Square, handle and spout in center of creamer side. Dark brown tile roof. Mark in orange with yellow sun "Cottage in the Sun. 1979 Enesco Imports Corp." Impressed, "Made in Japan." £9. $15 set.

129. **Japan** Teapot, 4 1/'2" high. Square, black and brown cottage. White door. "Japan." £15. $25.

130. **Japan** Creamer, brown and cream colored, 3" high. Square, with cornered handle and spout. Black window and door outlines. "Made in Japan."£12. $19.

131. **Japan** Mug, 5" high. Thatched cottage. Back has Japanese mountain scene. No mark. £9. $15.

132. **Japan** Creamer, 2 3/4" high. Square, dark brown, log cabin shape. Corner handle and spout. "Japan." £12. $19.

133. **Japan** Creamer, round, brick outlines, 2 1/2" high. Brown and cream colored, with dark brown and green accents. "Japan." £9. $15.

134. **Japan** Covered Sugar, 4" high. Square, cornered handles. Cream and brown colored with black outlines. "Made in Japan." £13. $25.

135. **Japan** Teapot. 6" high. Ivory colored, low relief, square low relief thatched cottage with greenery. "Japan." £30. $45.

136. **Japan** Covered Sugar, 4 1/4" high. Brown and cream colored thatched, brick cottage. Dark brown outlines. Cornered handles. No mark. £19. $29.

137. **Japan** Creamer, 3" high. Cottage, brick outlines. Cream colored and brown. Square, cornered handle and spout. No mark. £13. $25.

138. **Japan** Open Sugar or Jam Pot, 2 3/4" high. Brick or log cabin. Light brown and cream colored, white door. "Japan." £15. $25.

139. **Japan** Clock, 4 1/2" high. Quartz battery, brass outline. Grey bricked, Town Hall design, half-timbered on back side. Tiled roof, careful detailing. Felt covering on base covers mark. £19. $30.

140. **Japan** Clock, 5" high. Quartz battery. Tan and brown, black window outlines. Turrets. Careful attention to details. Felt covering on base covers mark. £19. $30.

141. **Japan** Lighter on attached base, 2 1/2" high. Brown thatched cottage, dark brown handle and outlines. No mark. £9. $15.

142. **Japan** Jug, 3" high, square brick cottage. Cream, dark green dark brown handle and outlines. "Made in Japan." £12. $19.

143. **Japan** Pastille Burner, 4 1/2" high x 6 1/2" wide. Red-tiled roof on tan building. Greenery, black outlined red door and windows. Unglazed, shows much use. c. 1920. Raised mark "Japan." £19. $29.

144. **Japan** Vase. 8" high, 3" wide. Two story building with green roof and "Sorority House" sign on front. A humorous collectible that would add a touch of fun to a townhouse collection. Female leaning out of second story window, tipsy serenader leaning against corner of house, both in relief. On paper sticker and impressed mark: JUON QUON Made in Japan. The date 1981 in Roman Numerals. £14. $29.

146. **Japan** Penny Bank, 6" high, brown, peaked roof, two-story house, red, white and blue trim, orange door. Impressed mark "Japan." £9. $20.

145. **Japan** Canister, 9 1/2" high Blue, brown roof and twin chimneys, white outlined windows. "Flour," sign above door. High glaze. Small sticker, "Made in Japan." £20. $35.

147. **Japan** Penny Bank, 6" high, gray, tile roof, two-story house. Orange door blue staircase. Impressed mark, "Japan." £14. $25.

148 through 152. **Japan** Canister Set. Some came with a folded tag: "The Townhouse Canister Collection." No other identification, except one of the boxes is stamped "Made in Japan." Pieces are all white. Only the fronts are marked with outline of a house in transfer pattern. The largest, a cookie jar, has painted outlines. Each has a sign to indicate use £75. $125 set.

148. **Japan** Sugar Canister, "Confectionery," 6 1/2" high. Blue front, tan roof, two-story. £20. $30.

150. **Japan** Coffee Container, "Coffee House," 5 1/2" high. One-story, basement windows green roof. £18. $25.

151. **Japan** Tea Caddy, "Tea Room," 6 1/2" high. Pink roof, yellow windows, pink-edged windows and door. £20. $25.

149. **Japan** Flour Canister. "Bakery," 9" high. Two-story, tan front, blue turreted roof. £29. $35.

152. **Japan** Cookie Jar, no label, 9" high. White, pink roof and window outlines. £21. $35

153 through 157. These are all part of the same set. Some have tiny red stickers marked "Made in Japan". Some have lost their sticker, but are easily recognized by their shape and coloring. There is a relief design on the front of each piece, with a continuing fence around each. Colorings are cream, orange, brown, and buttery yellow. Buildings have a golden yellow thatch. Usually seen separately, not as a set. £85. $135 set.

153. **Japan** Cookie Jar, 9 1/2" high. Low relief barn and part of house, with trees, a chicken, and a black and white cow. £23. $35.

154 and 155. **Japan** Covered Sugar, 5" high. Creamer, 3" high. £18. $25 set.

156. **Japan** Coffee or teapot, 7" high. Straight sides, more indicative of a coffee pot. Teapots are usually rounded. £23. $35.

157. **Japan** Covered Butter, 3 3/4" high, 7" long tray. £15. $19.

158, 159, 160, and 61. **Japan** Cups/Mugs, 3 1/2" high. Set of four. £7. $10 each.

162, and 163. **Japan** Salt and Pepper Shakers, 4" high. £13. $17 set.

164, and 165. **Japan** Salt and Pepper Shakers, 4" high. £12. $15 set.

165. **Made In Japan** Covered Jam Pot, 4 3/4" high. Round, with relief figures in front tiled area. Brightly colored, yellow, cream colored. At first glance, mark appears to be the same as other Made in Japan marks in half-circle, but on closer scrutiny is actually Murutamo Ware. Half circle mark with T in the center. £25. $50.

JOHNSON BROS. (England)

Johnson Bros, one of the Staffordshire potteries, has been in production in Hanley and Tunstall from 1883 to the present. It is still in operation as part of the Wedgwood Potteries. Village pieces are called Friendly Village, and include a printed description of the history of Johnson Bros.

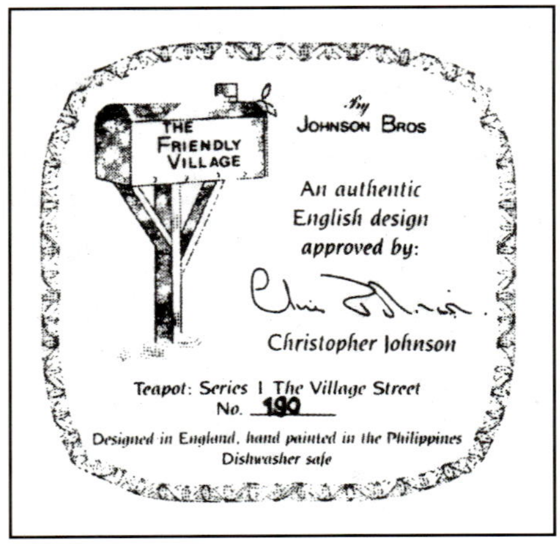

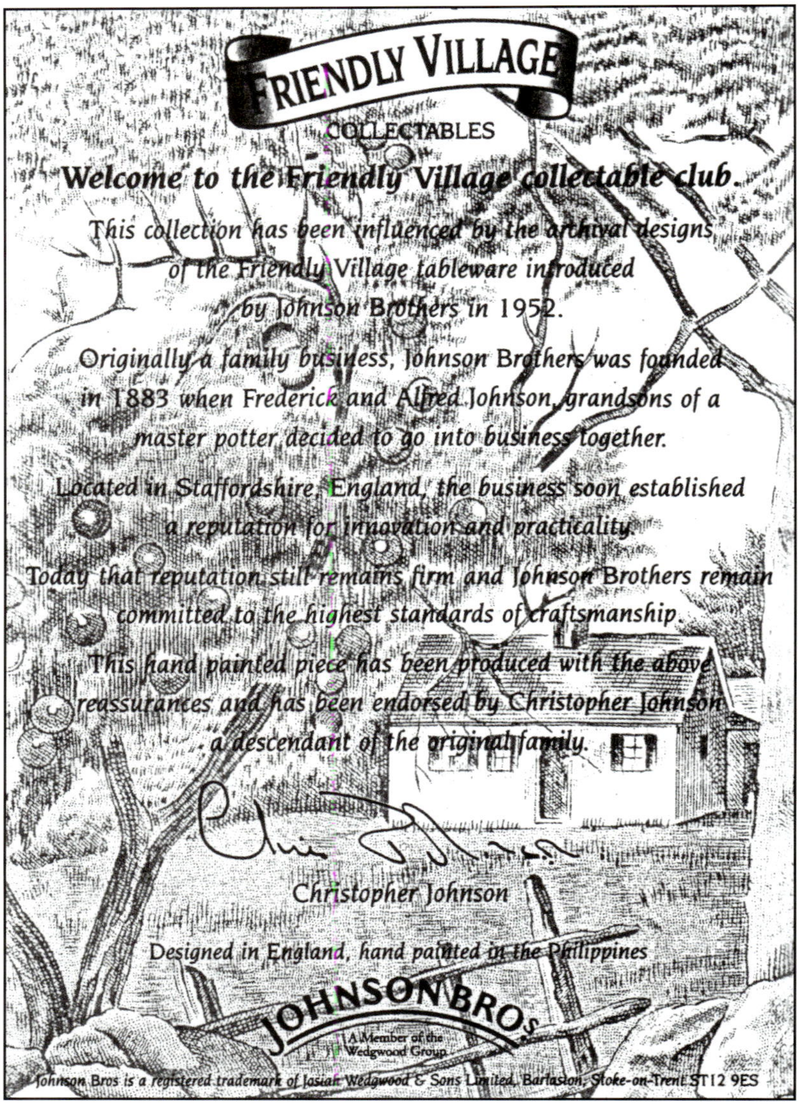

Johnson Bros. "Friendly Village" collectors club card and authenticity mark.

166. **Johnson Bros.** Teapot, white, brown, and green, 6" high. Two-story house, brown roof, green shrubbery. Descriptive backstamp. £55. $69.

JOSEF ORIGINALS (United States)

Josef Originals, begun by partners Muriel and Joseph George, operated from 1945 - 1985, when the company sold to a firm called Applause, which is still in operation. Known mostly for figurines and animals, with occasional novelty pieces.

167. **Josef Originals** Penny Bank, 5 1/4" high. White, with brown tiled roof, brown door, and greenery. $19.

KEELE STREET POTTERY CO (England)

Keele Street Pottery (KSP) was so named because they were located on Keele Street, in Tunstall, Staffordshire, from about 1913 - 1958, when they moved to Meir Airport, Longton. They were part of Staffordshire Potteries and produced earthenware. They were one of number of potteries known collectively as the Keele Street Pottery group. Keele St's cottages are easily recognizable for their square, thatched cottages with second-story windows that resemble square eyes with wide-spaced lashes. Color is somewhat muted, compared with others. Most carry the Keele St circle mark, although early pieces were not always marked and some marks have faded. Circa 1920s and 1930s.

Keele Street Pottery base marking

168. **Keele Street Pottery** Biscuit Barrel, 7 1/4" high to top of carrying handle. Cream-colored, tan, and brown, brown and beige handle. £75. $125.

169. **Keele Street Pottery** Cup and Saucer, 3 1/4" high across top of cup. Cottage is pictured on cup. Saucer has a cobbled street look. £15. $35.

170. **Keele Street Pottery** Trio—Cup, Saucer, Plate. Plate, 7" diameter, Cup, 3" high across top. Plate and Saucer have brown edge. £30. $49.

171. **Keele Street Pottery** Teapot, 5 1/4" high, light green and shades of brown. Brown thatched roof, handle, and spout. £40. $95.

172. **Keele Street Pottery** Condiment Set. Salt, Pepper, Toothpick Holder on square clover leaf tray. 3 1/2" high, tray 3 3/4" long. £60. $85.

173. **Keele Street Pottery** Match Holder, 2 3/4" high; base, 3 3/4" long. Holder opening in back, lower half of cottage door is the striker. Door and chimneys are rosey-colored. £40. $75.

174. **Keele Street Pottery** Coffee or Chocolate Pot, 7 1/2" high. Square, cornered handle and spout. £35. $85.

175. **Keele Street Pottery** Covered Butter, 4 3/4" high; Tray, 6". £38. $75.

176. **Keele Street Pottery** Teapot, 6 1/2" high. Square, handle and spout on side. £40. $85.

177. **Keele Street Pottery** Covered Sugar, 4 1/4" high. Square, handle and spout cornered. £35. $40.

178. **Keele Street Pottery** Covered Jam/Marmalade Pot, 4 1/2" high Opening for spoon, no handles. Square. £30. $50.

179. **Keele Street Pottery** Jug, 3" high. Square, corner handle and pouring spout. £30. $39.

180. **Keele Street Pottery** Covered Sugar, 4 1/2" high. No handles, square. £30. $35.

181. **Keele Street Pottery** Hot Water Jug, 6 1/2" high. Covered, square, cornered handle and pouring spout. £35. $65.

182. **Keele Street Pottery** Sugar, 2" high, open top, round, squared off corners for door. £20. $30.

183. **Keele Street Pottery** Creamer, 2 1/2" high, round, squared off corners for door. £20. $30.

184 through 186 appear to be part of a mini-tea set. Because they were not found together, they are listed separately.

184. **Keele Street Pottery** Teapot, 3 3/4" high, square. £38. $75

185. **Keele Street Pottery** Open Sugar, 1 3/4" high, round, no handles. £20. $35.

186. **Keele Street Pottery** Creamer, 2 1/2" high, round. £20. $35.

KENSINGTON (England)

Operated as Kensington Works, first in Henley, later in Burslem, from 1922 - 1937. Part of Staffordshire Potteries. Kensington joined with Price Bros in 1934, forming a new company, Price & Kensington. There appears to have been an overlap until 1961, with both names still being used. Kensington's backstamp was the Staffordshire knot with their initials inside the loops. Price & Kensington still holds the name Kensington. Before joining with Price Bros. Kensington had a different sort of coloring. Pieces are more muted, although rich, colors of green, orange, pink, rust, and pale yellow. Edgings are in brown.

Kensington Staffordshire knot base marking

188. **Kensington** Jam pot. £30. $65.

187. **Kensington** A pair of co-joined Covered Jam/Marmalade Pots, perched on a grassy hill on attached tray with yellow steps. 5" high; and 8" long across bottom. Unusual. Can be found in some English antique books. £58. $130.

189 **Kensington** Jam pot. £30. $65.

190 **Kensington** Teapot. £40. $95.

LANCASTER & SONS (England)

From 1900 - 1944, Lancaster & Sons operated as Dresdon Works, Henley. Part of Staffordshire Potteries, producing earthenware. Among their marks were L & S; L & Sons; and Lancaster. They became Lancaster & Sandland in 1944, which dates their cottage pieces to prior to that date. The backstamp has remained unchanged except for addition of numbers indicating year or model numbers. The backstamp on these pieces was used in the 1920s. There is almost no crazing or signs of wear, which would seem to indicate they were for display rather than use. The mark itself has faded over the years.

Lancaster & Sons base marking

191 and 192. Probably part of a condiment set with one shaker missing.

191. **Kensington** Mini-Mustard Pot 2" high. £20. $49.

192. **Kensington** Mini-Shaker, 3" high. £15. $40.

193. **Lancaster & Sons** Covered Cheese, 6 1/2" high. Pub, "Cheese Inn". White, black outlines, red-tiled roof with greenery. Red chimney. Green edged tray, 8 1/2" long. £65. $125

194. **Lancaster & Sons** Teapot, 5 1/4" high, on dark green-edged tray, 8 1/2" long. White, orange roof, green handle, black outlines. £40. $95.

LEFTON CHINA COMPANY (United States)

Lefton is a distributor of Japanese ceramics begun by George Z. Lefton after World War II. A Hungarian immigrant, he was instrumental in reviving the post-war Japanese ceramics industry. They are still in business. Although mostly known for figurines and novelty pieces, they also import a variety of dinnerware.

195. **Lefton China Company** Teapot, 5" high, tan, with brown thatched roof and accents. Has a brick effect. £29. $39.

LENOX CHINA (USA)

Lenox China has been a well-respected maker of fine china since it began operation in Langhorne, Pennsylvania in 1889. Lenox Collector's Club, a sideline and separate division of Lenox China, is a novelty mail-order collector's club begun in the 1980s, producing a series of collectibles. The Lenox Village (1982+) offered an entire range of kitchen and table ware, including household canisters and spice jars. Pieces depict an upscale, pastel-colored village of multi-story buildings. Roofs are grey, blue, tan, rust, yellow and green, some turreted. Shops are labeled, and include a bakery, tea shop, coffee shop, creamery, recipe house, and a set of small spice houses. There is also a village clock (a necessity from the days when a whole village told the time by the tolling of the church or town center clock, in days when every household could not afford a timepiece.

Ironically, even though they have been famous for mor than a century as makers of fine china and porcelain, the village pieces are marked, "Hand Crafted in Taiwan."

LENOX®
©LENOX
1991

HANDCRAFTED IN TAIWAN

The Lenox Village
Cookie Cottage
FINE PORCELAIN

Lenox base markings

196. **Lenox** Canister, "Tea," 7" high. £45. $65.

197. **Lenox** Cookie Jar, "Cookies," 11" high. £47. $75.

198. **Lenox** Canister, "Coffee," 9" high. £50. $70.

199. **Lenox** Recipe Holder, "Recipes," 5 1/2" high. £23. $35.

200. **Lenox** Clock, 5 3/4" high. Town Hall. £30. $55.

201. **Lenox** Salt and Pepper Shakers, 4" high, on brass handled stand, 5" long. £24. $40.

202. **Lenox** Canister, Sugar, "Confectionary," 5 1/2" high. £25 $40.

203. **Lenox** Creamer, "Creamery", 5 1/2" high. £25. $40.

204. **Lenox** Canister, Sugar "Confectionary", 5 1/2" high. £25. $40.

205. **Lenox** Spice Set. 24-piece set of spice jars, alphabetically marked, each one slightly different in design or color. Sold with specially made wooden display case with single drawer at bottom. Includes sugar spoon (ar right). Can be easily found individually. Spices include: Allspice, Basil, Bay, Celery, Chive, Cinnamon, Clove, Coriander, Dill, Garlic, Ginger, Marjoram, Mustard, Nutmeg, Oregano, Onion, Paprika, Parsley, Pepper, Rosemary, Saffron, Sage, Tarragon, and Thyme.
Spice Set, each one 4" high. Display Case 23" tall, 14 1/4" wide. Roof is wider. £150. $240 set.

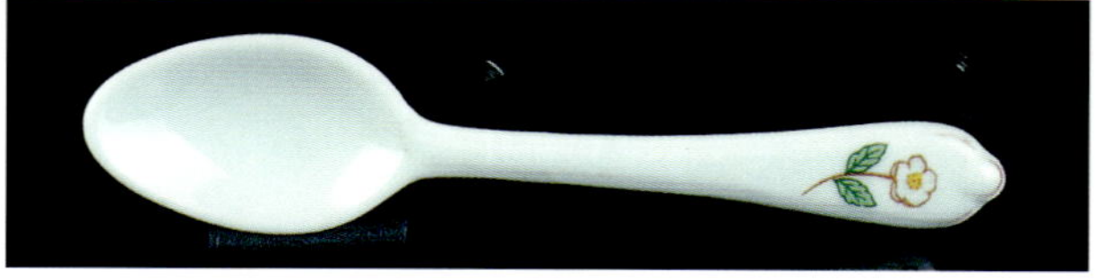

206. **Lenox** Sugar Spoon, 5". White with two-leafed yellow-centered flower painted at end. Gold mark, Lenox 1991. £10. $15.

JOHN MADDOCK & SONS (England)

Maddock began producing earthenware and ironstone pieces in Burslem in 1855. They were part of Staffordshire Potteries. Most of the pieces pictured have a similar look, rusty brown in color, with a darker overhanging thatched roofs, orange chimney, and dull green handles and foliage. An exception is one unmarked piece with different coloring: white with half-timbering mostly in black. Nearly all have a relief female figure standing in the doorway, and show signs of much use. Since the 1920s when the cottage series was first issued, Maddock's cottage ware has included identifying numbers on each piece—RD 742096 'Rustic'; and Reg'd. Shape 740521. Backstamps can be found in brown or green.

208. **Maddock** Teapot, 6" high x 9 1/2" wide, spout to handle. £40. $75.

Maddock base markings

210. **Maddock** Teapot, 4 1/4". 7" high, spout to handle. £45. $110.

207. **Maddock** Covered Sugar, 4 1/2" high, 6" wide roof. £40. $70.

211. **Maddock** Covered Jug, 4 1/4" high x 7" wide, spout to handle. £40. $100.

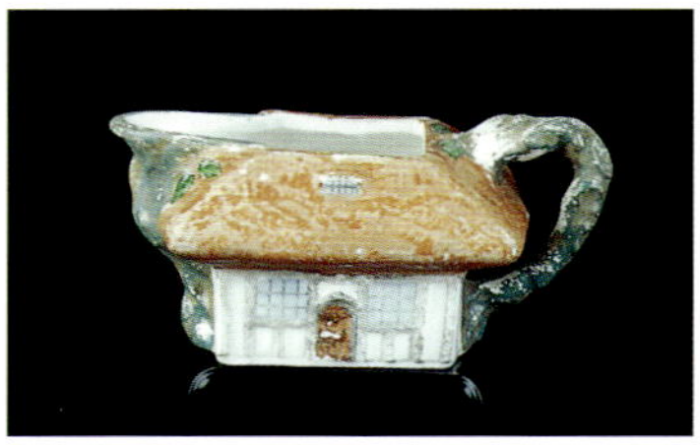

213. **Maddock** Mini-Creamer, 1 3/4" high. £35. $45.

212. **Maddock** Mini-Open Sugar, 2 1/4" high. £30. $45.

214. **Maddock** Teapot. Same design as other Maddock pieces, but different on roof, and glossy glass. Has a newer appearance with no signs of wear. Tan roof. £40. $100.

215. **Maddock** Covered Sugar.
4 1/4" high. £25. $40.

216. **Maddock** Cup, 2 1/2" high, Saucer, 5 1/2" diameter. £25. $30.

217. **Maddock** Condiment Set, 3 1/2" high on 6" long tray. £40. $75.

218. **Maddock** Creamer, 3" high, square, handle within the square. £23. $40.

219. **Maddock** Covered Jam Pot, 3 1/2" high. £25. $45.

220. **Maddock** Teapot, 6 1/2" high. £55. $95.

221. **Maddock** Condiment Set, 3 1/2" high on 6" long tray. Otherwise the same as #217 but darker colored. £35. $60.

222. **Maddock** Covered Butter or Cheese Dish. 5 1/2" high on 7" long tray. £28. $55.

McCOY (United States)

McCoy was in operation in Roseville, Ohio, from 1910 to 1980. It began as Nelson McCoy Sanitary Stoneware Company and produced necessary and practical houseware items. In the 1930s the name was changed to Nelson McCoy Pottery Company (later to shorten it to McCoy) and produced vases, cookie jars, and the like. McCoy is famous for their cookie jars, including several in cottage or village style. They ceased production in the 1980s. Not always marked or with a missing sticker.

Beware of modern imitations, including what appear to be exact copies of the original mark. These also come from Roseville, Ohio, and from Japan. Look for signs of age or use, and differences in color, if original pieces are what you seek.

223. **McCoy** Cookie Jar. Colored entirely in unglazed brown, including relief figure of female in Dutch costume in doorway. Exception: "Dutch Treat" painted in yellow, including plants, trim on roof, and milk can. 14" tall, probably the tallest piece in this book. No mark. £40. $85.

OCCUPIED JAPAN

Because the years of Allied occupation in Japan are a well-known part of history, this backstamp can easily be identified with a definite time span, after the devastation of World War II, when potteries re-tooled and resumed operation, to 1952 when the occupation ended and potteries went back to business as usual. This was not a quick or instant procedure, however, and some of the Japanese makers continued to use Japan or Made in Japan. Because of the circumstances of the war, Japan was not a popular mark with the U.S. and England, so 'Foreign' was sometimes used because it was not readily associated with Japan. As memories of the horrors of war faded, Japan resumed business with their old backstamp, Made in Japan.

Many of the Occupied Japan pieces are nearly identical to English cottage ware, especially to those made by Price-Kensington. Some have the same half-circle mark with Made in Occupied Japan and a T within a circle.

225. **Made in Occupied Japan** Pastille Burner. Orange tiled roof, two-story building. Souvenir of Yellowstone" sign on top of roof. Double door, round opening in back for flame. 4" high, 5" wide. Raised letters "Made in Occupied Japan". Unglazed. £25. $35.

Occupied Japan base marking

224. **Made in Occupied Japan** Covered Jam Pot. Round, 4" high. Cream colored, yellow trim and roof. Has a three-line mark. £30. $45.

226. **Made in Occupied Japan** Pastille Burner. Brown two-story building, 3 1/2" high, 4 3/4" wide. Red roof, blue chimney, yellow tiles on lean-to. Round opening in back. Unglazed. £27. $39.

PARAMOUNT (England)

Not a great deal of information is to be found about Paramount. They produced earthenware from 1946, first at Hanley, later at Meir Airport, Longton. They were part of Staffordshire Potteries. There are two different marks on these pieces, one circular, the other straight, possibly indicative of time frame, although it was not unheard of for a pottery to use more than one mark at a time, depending on series of production.

Paramount base markings

228. **Paramount** Biscuit barrel. 7" high, 10" high to top of brown and yellow wrapped handle. Square, cream-colored, pink flowers over door, dark brown outlines. £45. $110.

227. **Paramount** Covered Butter, 5" high, 6" long tray. Green, orange, and yellow thatched cottage. Green door, brown outlines. £40. $75.

229. **Paramount** Covered Butter, 5" high, 6" long tray. Cream and brown thatched cottage. £50. $75.

PHILIPPINES

It is occasionally possible to find a piece of cottage ware marked Philippines, probably made there for a U.S. distributor.

Philippines Strata Group base marking

Price Bros. base markings

230. **Philippines** Covered Butter. Rectangular, 4" high on 8" long tray. Brown, thatched roof cottage. Yellow, pink, green flowers. Strata Group. $45.

231. **Price Bros.** Teapot, 6" high. Green-roofed log cabin. Brown with greenery. £30. $95.

PRICE BROS. (England)

Crown Works, Burslem, Staffordshire. Price Bros. produced earthenware from the lates 1800s - 1934, when they merged with Kensington to become Price & Kensington. Some references note that this occured in 1961, but present-day Price Kensington catalogs are printed "Established in 1934." This makes it apparent that a backstamp of Price Bros. or Kensington would date a piece to the years before 1934, but there was probably an overlap until 1961 or so. The Price Bros. backstamp was a circle of leaves with "Price Bros." printed within the circle. Price Kensington kept the same backstamp with the addition of the name Kensington.

Most Price Bros. pieces are brick cottages with similar colors of brown, cream-colored, and greenery. All with same or similar design and coloring. Any variations will be described.

232. **Price Bros.** Toast Rack, 3" high, 4" wide. Three-slice, green, brown and cream-colored. £20. $45.

233. **Price Bros.** Egg Cups (4) 2" high, with greenery at base. Round, on 5 1/4" long tray, handled, with square indentations for the four cups. Brown and white tray. £25. $65.

234. **Price Bros.** Salt and Pepper Shakers, 3" high. No tray. £20. $45.

235. **Price Bros.** Jug, 7 1/2" tall, bright yellow, in relief. Cottage at end of path with grass, flowers, and trees. £49. $165.

236. **Price Bros.** Biscuit Barrel, 10" high to top of handle. Wrapped brown and dark green handle. £55. $125.

237. **Price Bros.** Teapot, 6 1/2" high. £45. $110.

238. **Price Bros.** Covered Butter, 5" high on 6 1/2" long tray. £45. $75.

239. **Price Bros.** Mug, 5" high. £20. $45.

240. **Price Bros.** Teapot, 5" high. £55. $110.

241. **Price Bros.** Covered Sugar, Square, 4" high. £35. $55.

242. **Price Bros.** Creamer, square, handle within the square, 3" high. £25. $35.

244. **Price Bros.** Covered Jam Pot, 4" high. £25. $75.

243. **Price Bros.** Condiment Set. Salt, Pepper, and Mustard in middle. 4" high, on 6 1/2" long tray. £30. $75.

245. **Price Bros.** Covered Jam Pot, 4" high. £25. $75.

PRICE & KENSINGTON, (England)

Price & Kensington was formed in 1934 from two potteries, Price Bros and Kensington. They produced everyday kitchen and table ware, including a steady production of cottage ware, into the present. After the merge they continued to use the old Price Bros mark with the addition of Kensington, becoming Price & Kensington within a circle of leaves. The cottage ware seems to be made from the old Price Bros molds.

Over time, Price Kensington has probably made more cottage ware than all other English potteries combined because theirs has been a steady output, rather than occurring over a few year span. Most have the same coloring, with few variations. One line of teapot, cream, sugar, cup and saucer is all white, contrasted by dark brown window and door outlines and half-timber markings. Another is a white covered butter with a bright red roof, and still another is a green and brown log cabin.

Price & Kensington Potteries base marking

Price & Kensington Potteries, Ltd. advertising piece

Price & Kensington catalog page, 1999.

246 - 252. These white pieces all have the same white coloring, with pink flowers. They appear to have been made from the same mold used for their other, more highly colored, pieces.

246. **Price & Kensington** Biscuit Barrel, white, 9" high to top of handle. £45. $95.

247. **Price & Kensington** Covered Butter, white, 5" high on 6 1/2" long tray. £25. $55.

248. **Price & Kensington** Teapot, white, 6" high. £40. $95.

249, and 250. **Price & Kensington** Cream, 6" high, Sugar, 4" high. White, square, handle on corner. £35. $65 set.

251. **Price & Kensington** Cup and Saucer, white. £20. $35 set.

252. **Price & Kensington** Tray, 6" long, for small teapot or covered butter. Regular brown and yellow coloring. £10. $25.

253. **Price & Kensington** Covered Butter, 5" high, on 6" long tray. Bright red roof and tray. Unusual. £35. $55.

254. **Price & Kensington** Teapot, 5" high. £35. $75.

255. **Price & Kensington** Coffee Pot, 6 1/2" high. £35. $85.

256. **Price & Kensington**
Teapot, 6 1/2" high. £35. $85.

257. **Price & Kensington** Cup and Saucer. £15. $35.

258. **Price & Kensington**
Teapot, 5 1/2" high. £35. $75.

259. **Price & Kensington** Bell, 4 1/2" high. £15. $35.

261. **Price & Kensington** Salt and Pepper, 3 1/4" high. £20. $40.

260. **Price & Kensington** Penny Bank, 5" high. £25. $45.

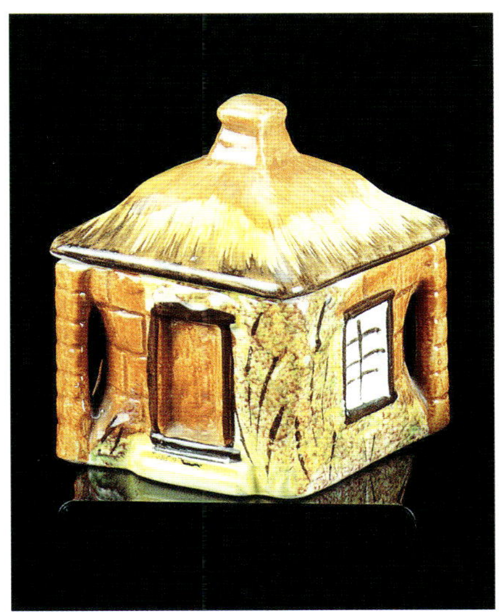

262. **Price & Kensington** Covered Sugar, 4 1/2" high. £20. $45.

263. **Price & Kensington**
Creamer, 3" high. £15. $35.

264. **Price & Kensington**
Mug, 4" high. £15. 40.

265. **Price & Kensington**
Container/Canister, 9" high.
£30. $75.

266. **Price & Kensington** Covered Butter, 5" high on 6 1/2" long tray. £30. $75.

267. **Price & Kensington** Container/Canister, 7 1/2" high. £30. $65.

268. **Price & Kensington** Jug, Relief, 7 1/2" high. Man on horseback in front of building. £85. $175.

269. **Price & Kensington** Condiment Set of three pots on 8" long tray. £30. $75.

270. **Price & Kensington** Toast Rack, 4-slice. £30. $75.

271. **Price & Kensington** Creamer, 3" high, cornered spout and handle. £15. $40.

272. **Price & Kensington** Covered Sugar, 4 1/4" high, no handles. £15. $40.

273. **Price & Kensington** Covered Butter Box, 4 1/2" high, 5" long. £20. $45.

274. **Price & Kensington** Egg Cups on square tray with indentations. Egg Cups, 2" high, tray, 6" long. £30. $65.

RAINBOW (United States)

This piece is included as a modern example. Rainbow is probably a distributing company, not a pottery.

REGENCY ROW (United States)

Another example of a modern piece produced for a distributor.

275. **Rainbow** Cookie Jar, 13" high. Painted decal design only on front. Tree story. "Bake Shop" sign across the top of first floor window. Tan roof, green shutters, brown door. Impressed mark, "Rainbow 1994." £30. $55.

276. **Regency Row** Container/Canister, 10 1/2" high. Octagonal shape. Three panels on front form the building facade. Golden brown color, three stories. Sign in front "Flour." Marked on bottom in black letters "Regency Row by JBC." $35.

ROYAL WINTON (England)

Royal Winton began operation in 1885, in Stoke, Staffordshire, England, as Grimwade Bros. It was founded by brothers Laurence and Sidney Grimwade. As with other early potteries, they were known for their everyday utility household ware. Their cottage ware, made in the 1920s and 1930s, is the front-runner in relief, detail, depth of color, and realistic design. Compared with some, their pieces are works of art; others are pale imitations. They are still operating, although the Grimwade family ceased ownership in the 1960s.

Reportedly, the Queen found Royal Winton's cottage ware amusing enough to order for use in the Royal Household. Royal Winton has many collectors, as do Beswick, Burlington, and other English potteries of the same era and similar calibre. Royal Winton made several series of cottage pieces with same mark: Ye Olde Inn; Olde England; Ye Olde England; Ye Olde Mill. Some had a circle or straight line Royal Winton mark, some were marked only Made in England; still others had no mark at all. Their cottage ware covers a wide range and pieces differ somewhat in color and style. All are collectible.

277. **Royal Winton** Biscuit Barrel, 9" high to top of handle. Three-story Pub. Mauve tiled roof, sign above door has a swan. Blue windows, brown handle, dark brown outlines. Mark on bottom "Ye Olde Inn." £95. $185.

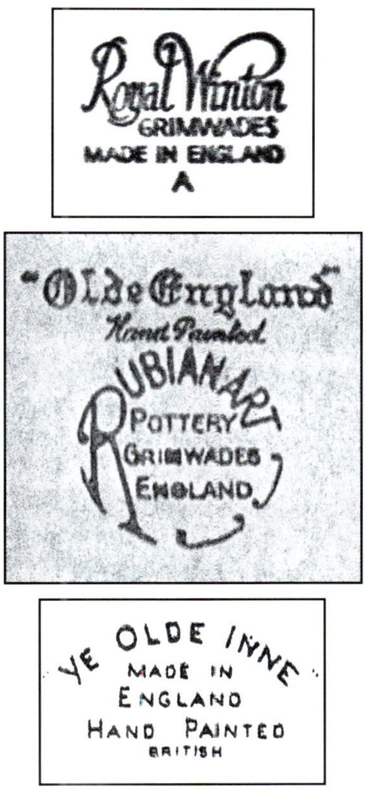

Royal Winton base markings

278. **Royal Winton** Open Jam Pot, 2 3/4" high. Pink flowers over door and window, black outlines. Mark on bottom: "Made in England", no maker's mark. £35. $95.

The Royal Winton International Collectors' Club

REFERENCE LIBRARY No. 12 in a series

GRIMWADES LTD. :: STOKE-ON-TRENT

(Incorporating Rubian Art Pottery & Atlas China)

"Ye Old Inne"

Table Novelty

(Hand-painted).

A splendid example of the Pottery Modellers craft, which combined with the skill of specially trained artists faithfully depicts a feature of rural England in the old coaching days.

Item No.		Price per dozen
1.	Cruet, 3 pieces on Tray	**27/-**
2.	Covered Butter	**24/-**
3.	Condiment Set (Salt & Pepper on Tray) ...	**21/-**
4.	Marmalade and Stand	**21/-**
5.	Sugar, 2½" diameter	**36/-** per doz. prs.
8.	Cream, 8 ozs. capacity ...	
6.	Sugar Sifter	**15/-** per dozen
7.	Dessert Plate, 8¼" diameter ...	**16/-** per dozen

Item No.		Price per dozen
8.	See item 5 for price.	
9.	Covered Jug, 15 ozs. capacity	**28/-**
10.	Open Jug, 15 ozs. capacity	**21/-**
11.	Cheese	**36/-**
12.	Covered Biscuit, with Wicker handle ...	**39/-**
13.	Teapot, 33 ozs. capacity	**36/-**
	and Teapot Stand	**12/-**

Can also supply :—

Bulb Bowl, Oblong ... ... **48/-** per dozen

Length 10¼", Width 6", Depth 3½"

Royal Winton International Collectors' Club and Grimwades Ltd. Advertisement.
Courtesy of Ken Glibbery, London, International Chintz Club.

279. **Royal Winton** Covered Cheese, 6 1/2" high, on green tray, 7 1/2" long. Mauve tiled roof. Marked "Ye Olde Inn." £85. $135.

280. **Royal Winton** Teapot, 5 3/4", plain white, and unusual, since they are known for their coloring. Unpainted pieces of cottage ware are hard to find. Marked "Olde England" and "Rubian Art." £45. $85.

281. **Royal Winton** Covered Jam Pot, 5" high, on 5" square tray. Yellow thatch, blue windows, black outline. £65. $130.

282. **Royal Winton** Salt and Pepper, 2 3/4" high, no tray. Half-timbered, brown outlines. No marks. £35. $75.

283. **Royal Winton** Covered Butter, 4 1/4" square on 5 ¾" long green-edged tray, pink flowers at corners. Yellow thatch with greenery, pink flowers. A different design. Royal Winton circular mark. £95. $170.

284. **Royal Winton** Biscuit Barrel, 9" high to top of brown and green wrapped handle. Yellow thatch, half-timbered, flowers by door of yellow cottage. Marked "Ye Olde England." £90. $175..

285. **Royal Winton** Plate, 8 1/2" diameter. Thatched cottage on road with picket gate and low wall enclosing a country garden. Marked "Olde England." £95. $175.

286. **Royal Winton** Tankard, 6 1/2" high. Twisted relief handle. Outline of village houses on one side, relief dancing figures on other. Yellow, green, brown. Circular Royal Winton mark. £125. $250.

287. **Royal Winton** Teapot, 6" high, dark brown, green, yellow, and orange. Pub with faded sign "Ye Olde Swan," pink flowers above door. Circle Royal Winton mark. £120. $195.

288. **Royal Winton** Condiment Set: Salt, Pepper, Mustard, 3" high on 5 1/4" long tray. Mustard-colored thatch on cottages. Square, clover-leaf light green tray. Marked "Olde England." £95. $165.

289. **Royal Winton** Coffee Pot, 6 1/2" high. Cornered handle and spout, door in corner. Black outlines. Marked "Ye Olde Inne." £75. $145.

290. **Royal Winton** Open Jam Pot, 3" square, Pub with swan above door. Yellow, black outlines, greenery. Marked "Ye Olde Inne." £35. $95.

291. **Royal Winton** Hot Water Jug, 4 1/2" high, top missing. Red tiled roof edge, three-story, much greenery. Faded mark, "Made in England." £45. $105.

292. **Royal Winton** Jug, 4 1/2" square, with cornered handle and spout. Green, cream, blue windows. Marked "Olde England." £55. $110.

293. **Royal Winton** Cake Plate, two-tiers, 8 1/2" diameter each. Half-timbered Tudor Pub. Two-story with attic window in relief. Swan sign in front. Mauve tiled roof. £110. $225.

294. **Royal Winton** Jug, 3 1/2" high, cream colored with greenery, black door and outlines. Pink flowers. Marked, "Made in England." £45. $75.

295. **Royal Winton** Biscuit Barrel, 9 1/2" high to top of handle. Red-tiled roof, mill wheel behind cottage. Two-story, blue windows, cottage is covered with green vines. £90. $165.

296. **Royal Winton** Covered Cheese, 5 1/2" high on 7 1/2" high green tray. Red tiled roof, mill wheel behind cottage. Double brown swinging doors on front, red flowers. No mark. £85. $195.

297. **Royal Winton** Teapot, 5 1/2" high, lighter colored, greens, browns, cream. Flowers in front. Square, handle and spout cornered, with door in corner. Black and red chimney, dark brown handle and spout. Has straight line Royal Winton mark. £85. $195.

298. **Royal Winton** Jug, 5". Lighter-colored, cream, green, brown, tan thatch. Has straight line Royal Winton mark. £75. $175.

299. **Royal Winton** Teapot, 6" square. Handle and spout cornered. Black and red double chimney, dark brown handle and spout. £75. $175.

300. **Royal Winton** Sugar Shaker, 6" high. Dark blue windows, dark brown outlines, red enameled flowers. No marks. £55. $125.

301. **Royal Winton** Sugar Shaker, 6" high. Yellow, green, cream, with greenery and orange outlines. Yellow window and door. No marks. £55. $125.

SADLER (England)

Sadler was part of Staffordshire Potteries, producing earthenware pieces fron 1899 to the present in Burslem, Staffordshire. They are noted as a teapot manufacturer, with special issues from time to time, including historic or notable English houses and builings. Most designs are transfer ware. The company is not known for relief ware. Ironically, one of those pictured was made in China and is so marked. Their Potter piece is especially interesting because it has the story of the potter on the bottom, and the potter's home/workplace is on front and back.

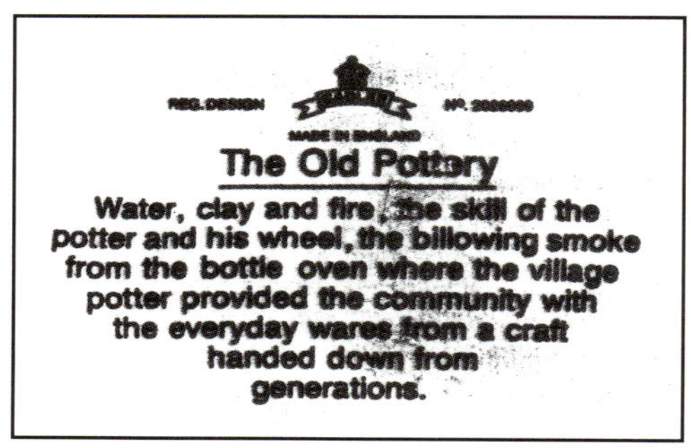

302. **Royal Winton** Teapot, 6" high. Square, handle and spout cornered. Brown handle and spout. £85. $175.

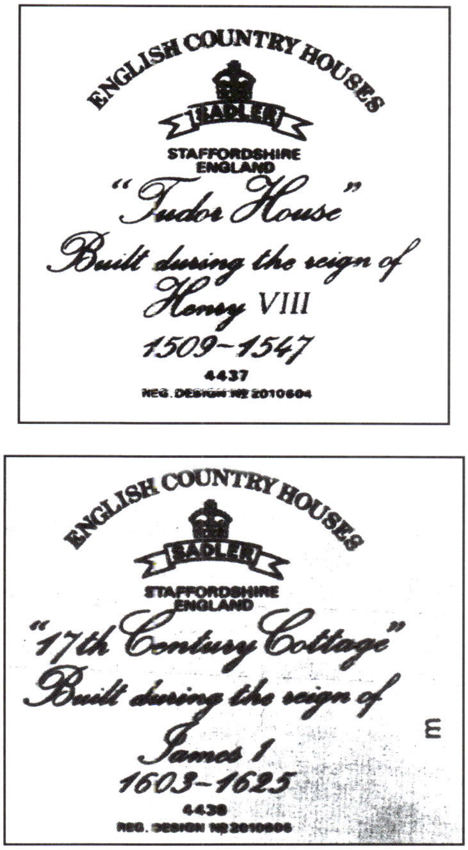

Sadler base markings

303. **Sadler** Tea Caddy, 5" high. Marked "HB Teahouse" or front. Brown roof, two yellow doors, brown, white, blue windows. Part of a group of teapots depicting English houses of different periods. Carries the Sadler mark and Made in China. Also marked "Wellington." £46. $60.

304. **Sadler** Teapot, 6 1/2" high. Image of a Pub with sign on front, "Ye Olde Tea Pot Inn." A man holding a glass of beer stands in the open doorway. Marked "Sadler Made in England." £30. $75.

305. **Sadler** Teapot, 6" high. Brown and white, tan tiled and gabled roof. Part of English country house series. Marked "Tudor House." £25. $85.

306. **Sadler** Teapot, 6" high. The number 1620 is shown above the door. Vari-colored bricks. Marked "17th Century Cottage." £35. $75.

307. **Sadler** Teapot, 6 1/2" high, depicts pot bank, both front and back. Vari-colored bricks and roof tiles. Potter is shown in front of door with a pile of coal. Fire from kiln shows inside other entrance. On bottom is the story of the potter. £25. $75.

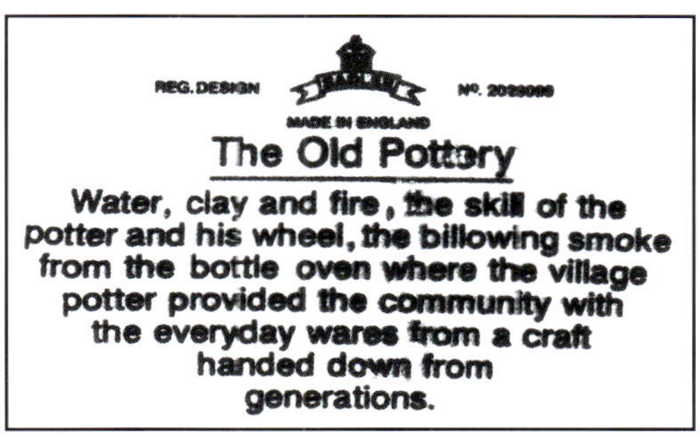

Markings on the base of the pot bank.

SEARS, ROEBUCK AND COMPANY
(United States)

All four pieces of this canister set have the same mark, indicating they were part of the original set. All are creamy white, with different roof lines, styles, and purposes. All are marked SEARS, ROEBUCK AND CO, 1981 Made in Japan.

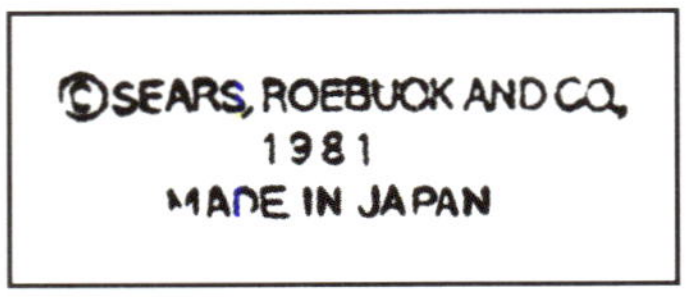

Sears, Roebuck and Co.
base marking

308. **Sears Roebuck and Company**
Canister/Container, 9" high. "Sugar" on front. Blue tile roof, red chimney. £23. $40.

309. **Sears Roebuck and Company**
Canister/Container, 8 1/2" high. "Coffee" on front. Orange-brown tile roof. No chimney. £20. $35.

310. **Sears Roebuck and Company**
Canister/Container, 7 1/2" high. "Tea" on front. Orange chimney, green tile roof. £20. $35.

311. **Sears Roebuck and Company** Canister/ Container in the shape of a mill and marked "Flour." 11" high. Yellow thatch, shuttered windows. £24. $45.

312. **Shorter & Son Ltd.** Covered Jam Pot, 5 1/2" high. Round, brown-black door, brown thatch. Greenery, blue many-paned windows. Carries Shorter mark. £45. $75.

SHORTER & SON LTD (England)

Shorter is located on Copeland Street, in Stoke, Staffordshire. They have produced earthenware pieces since 1909, and were part of Staffordshire Potteries.

Shorter & Son Ltd.
base markings

313. **Shorter & Son Ltd.** Covered Butter Dish, 4"high on 7 1/4" long shaped tray. Round, relief pink and yellow flowers. Marked Shorter. *Courtesy of Shirley and Klaus Mendenhall.* £45. $85.

314. **Shorter & Son Ltd.** Biscuit Barrel, six-sided, 9 1/2" high to top of brown handle. Brown rooster perched on top of lid. Rounded base. Dark blue windows with black outlines, dark green door. £85. $165.

315. **Shorter & Son Ltd.** Covered Butter/Cheese, 7" high on 8" long tray. Brown Log Cabin. Dark brown accents and door. Flower boxes. Slight differences from the similar Beswick log cabin. No mark. £45. $95.

SYLVA/CERNO (England)

SylvaC began as Shaw & Copestake Ltd. Also known as SylvaC Works it was in operation from 1901 to 1982. They produced earthenware as part of Staffordshire Potteries. In 1957, they opened a new factory, SylvaCeramics. Sylvan Works (Longton) and Copestake combined, shortening the name to SylvaC. This would date their cottage pieces to after 1957. Cottage pieces with the SylvaC backstamp are hard to find. Two jam pots are identical in appearance to the covered butter dish, but the butter dish is marked SylvaC and the jam pots are marked CERNAC. The pieces shown were purchased in different areas—two in Washington (state) and the teapot in Canada. All appear identical, but have different marks.

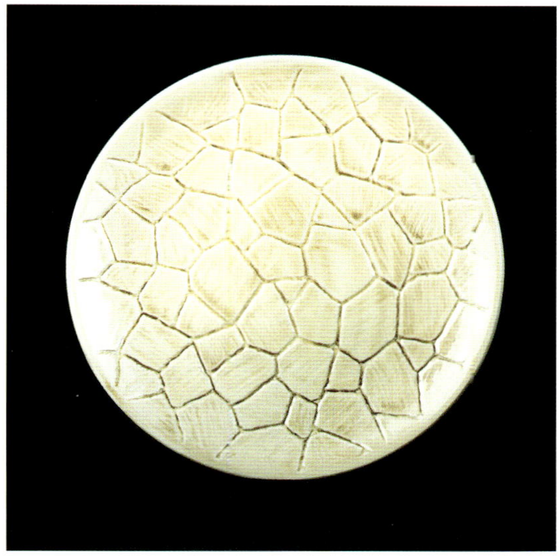

317. **Sylva / Cerno** Plate, 6" diameter. Cobbled, no design, no mark, but matches tray in color and design. £10. $35.

Sylva/Cerno base markings

316. **Sylva / Cerno** Covered Butter, 4 1/2" high, on Tray, 6 1/2" long. Cream/white with dark outlines. Tan thatch, blue windows, pink and green relief flowers. Green door, cobbled tray. Marked Sylva Ceramics. £45 $110.

318. **Sylva / Cerno** Covered Sugar, 5" high. Square, no handles, pink and green relief flowers. Marked CERNO Made in England. £45. $75.

319. **Sylva / Cerno** Creamer, 3" high. Square, pink and green relief flowers. Marked CERNO Made in England. £30. $65.

STAFFORDSHIRE CROFT (England)

Research turned up nothing about this backstamp, and only a few pieces, but they are interesting, and good examples of cottage ware. It seems probable that this is another example of a short-lived pottery, perhaps part of Staffordshire Potteries.

Staffordshire Croft base marking

320. **Staffordshire Croft** Covered Jam Pot, 5" high. Round, tan brick cottage. Green door, tan thatch, brown outlines, pink relief flowers. Marked "Staffordshire Croft." £35. $55.

321. **Staffordshire Croft** Teapot, 6" high. Round, yellow thatch, green door, brown outlines. Pink relief flowers. No maker's mark. £55. $95.

322. **Staffordshire Croft** Covered Jam Pot, 5" high. Round, tan brick cottage. Tan thatch, brown outlines, green door, pink relief flowers. £35. $55.

TAIWAN

Taiwan is an island, formerly Formosa, that belonged to Japan from 1895 until 1945. It is now part of the Republic of China. Taiwan produces and exports a variety of goods to various parts of the world. Some examples are included to add to the variety of modern design in pieces pictured in the book.

BENJAMIN & MEDWIN INC.N.Y.N.Y.
©'58, '66 UFS, INC.
MADE IN TAIWAN

Taiwan Benjamin & Medwin Inc. base marking

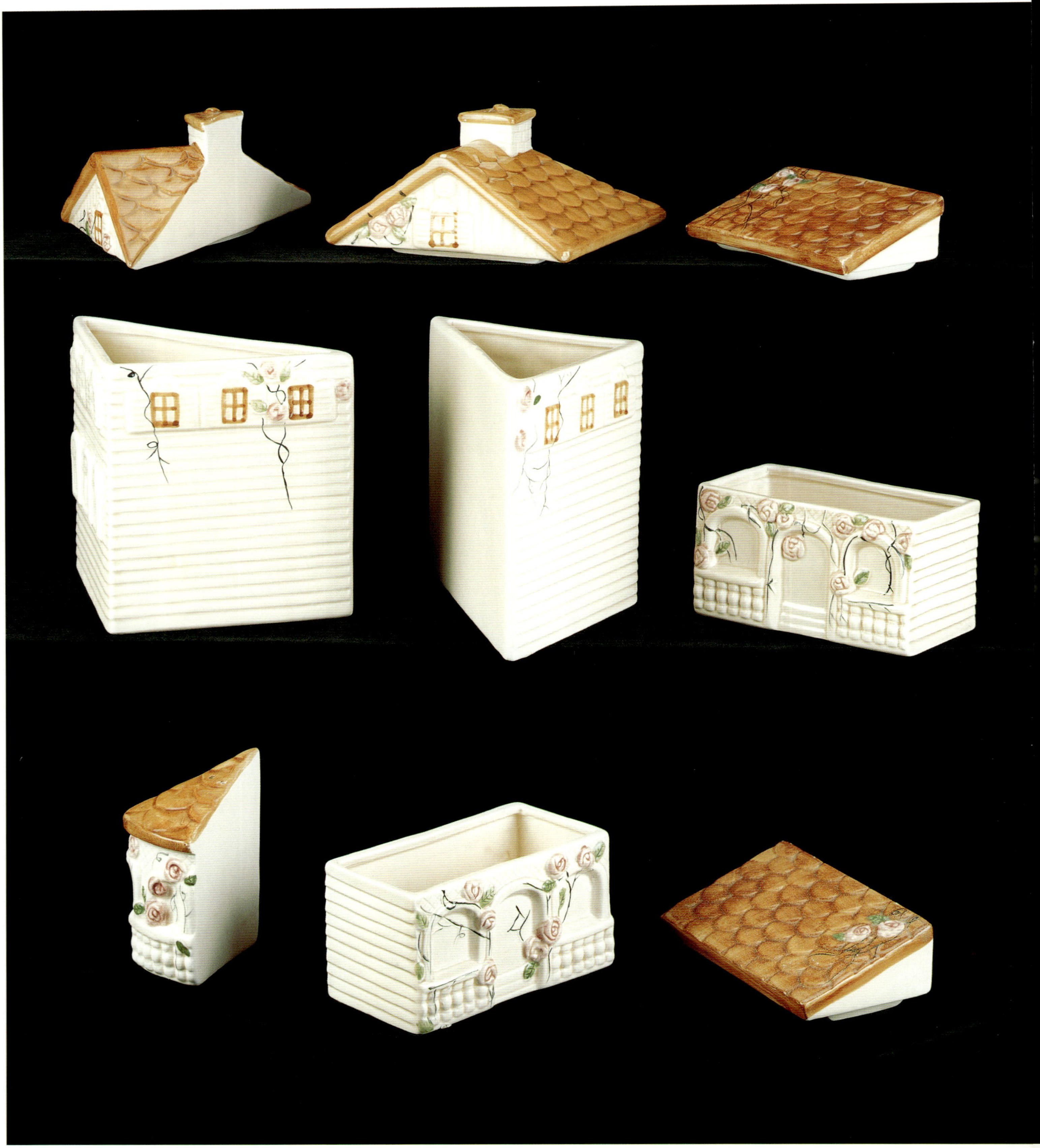

323. **Taiwan** Canister Set, unassembled. 11 pieces including lids. There should be 12 pieces, but one shaker is missing. Two-story house is basically in two architectural parts. The main house is 10" high, with two 5" high additions. Salt and pepper shakers fit into the shape to make still another.

324. **Taiwan** Canister Set assembled to make a smart-looking, two-story, tiled-roof, country house. Creamy beige, brown roofs. Pink flowering vines (one shaker missing). £39. $110.

TREASURE CRAFT (United States)

Treasure Craft began operation in Pasadena, California, in the 1940s, and is still in business today under the ownership of Pfaltzgraff Potters. They feature novelty pieces as well as kitchen and household ware, especially cookie jars.

325. **Treasure Craft** Cookie Jar, 10 1/2" high. Haunted House. Victorian style, two-story house with dull yellow hooded windows. Brown, red chimney, relief stairway in front. Unglazed. No marks. £30. $75.

326. **Treasure Craft** Cookie Jar, 12" high. Yellow, brown tiled roof. Raised mark on bottom of front, "Treasure Craft USA." £30. $65.

TWIN WINTON (United States)

Twin Winton was founded in 1936 by twins Ross and Don Winton, in Pasadena, California. Known for animal figures and novelty pieces, including cookie jars. Ceased operation to enlist in the military during World War II, then returned to business in 1946, after the war, moving to increasingly larger premises. Still in business today, under ownership of Treasure Craft since the 1970s.

327. **Twin Winton** Cookie Jar, 14" high. All brown, including chimney. Unglazed, yellow outlines. Sign, "Cookie Barn" on front. Relief animal heads at openings—pig, lamb, chicken, horse. Inside cream-glaze. No mark. £35. $75.

WADE / WADEHEATH (England)

Early records of Wade show its beginning in Burslem, Staffordshire, in 1810. It became George Wade & Son in 1919, and the WADEHEATH from 1927 to 1970. Wade is a favorite of collectors who seek out their miniature houses, cottages, castle, and such, which, along with miniature animal figures, is what they are known for. In the 1970s they produced a series called Whimseys. In 1984, the Whimsey idea was used to create novelty kitchen storage jars in the form of village shops for storing tea, coffee, sugar and cheese, some made especially for food distributors as mail-in premium items. (Salada Tea, Canada) Some of the Village Store series are shown here. Basically, these are white boxes with transfer designs on the front only, and identical in size. Shop names are printed in front to indicate the container's use. Roofs are different colors for individuality. An exception is a Cheese Shop, a covered cheese keep. It has relief detail and is much more appealing.

Wade base marking

Wadeheath base marking

No. 312-1. "YE OLDE TEA ROOM"—Tea Caddy.
No. 313-2. "THE COFFEE HOUSE"—Coffee Storage Jar.
No. 314-3. "B. LOAF, BAKER & CAKES"—Flour Storage Jar.
No. 315-4. "MRS. SMITH, ICE CREAM & SWEETS"—Sugar Storage Jar.
All storage jars measure 7½″ from base to top of chimney and are 3⅝″ square. All four containers are marked "Village Stores by WADE Staffordshire ENGLAND."
No. 316-5. "THE CHALK AND CHEESE"—The Covered Cheese Dish. The white base is 7¼″ long by 5¼″ wide and 11/16″ deep. The base is unmarked. The house, in the design of an English Pub, is 5″ high by 6¼″ long by 4⅜″ wide and is marked on the inside face of the back wall "Village Stores by WADE Staffordshire ENGLAND."
No. 317-6. "THE VILLAGE STORE POST OFFICE"—The Covered Butter Dish. The base and lid combined measures 5″ high, the roof being the removable lid. The base measures 5¼″ long by 3¾″ wide and is marked on the underside "Village Stores by WADE Stafforshire ENGLAND."
No. 318-7. "POST OFFICE"—Salt Shaker (small size).
No. 319-8. "POST OFFICE, ROYAL MAIL"—Pepper Shaker (small size).
Both shakers are from the same mold but with a different design even though both depict a Post Office. The houses measure 2⅛″ high by 1¼″ long by 1″ wide. Both are marked "WADE ENGLAND" on the face of the back wall.
No. 320-9. "A. SALT, GREENGROCER"—Salt Shaker (large size).
No. 321-10. "B. PEPPER, FAMILY BUTCHER"—Pepper Shaker (large size).

Wade Village Stores model numbers

328. **Wade** Canister/Container, 7 1/2". "Baker Loaf Cakes' is printed on brown across front over windows showing bakery display with a baker and a customer. Blue windows, chocolate brown roof. £20. $40.

329. **Wade** Canister/Container, 7 1/2" high. "The Coffee House" printed in yellow across the front. Yellow and white canopy over door. Light brown roof. £20. $40.

330. **Wade** Canister/Container, 7 1/2" high. "Ye Olde Tearoom" printed across front. Black half-timbers. Many paned windows. Grey-blue roof. £20. $40.

331. **Wade** Canister/Container, 7 1/2" high. "Ice Cream Mrs. Smith Sweets" printed in green across front. Blue second story windows with window boxes. £20. $40.

332. **Wadeheath** Biscuit Barrel, 6 1/2" high. Knobby looking relief, un-handled. Yellow and brown with brown outlines, relief flowers. Circa 1930s. £50. $95.

333. **Wade** Covered Cheese Keeper, 6 1/2" high, on white 7 1/2" long tray. White, thatched pub. "Chalk and Cheese" sign above door. Unmarked. £30. $60.

334, 335, and 336. **Wade** These are part of the same set, white, with similar transfer designs on all four sides.

334. **Wade** Creamer, 2 1/2" high. "Village Dairy" sign across front. "Village Milk Jug" is repeated on protruding lip at bottom of piece on all sides. No marks. £25. $40.

335. **Wade** Covered Sugar, 4" high. "Sweet Sue's Sweet Shop Hand Made Confection" sign on front. "A sweet shop sugar bowl" is repeated on protruding lip at bottom of piece on all sides. Marked on bottom "English Life Designs by Barry Smith and Barbara Wootton Exclusively for WADE England." £20. $40.

336. **Wade** Teapot, 6" high. "Antiques" sign on front. Slate gray tiled roof with white and cobalt blue accents. "An Antique Teapot" is repeated on protruding lip at bottom of piece on all sides. Same marking on bottom as #335. £45. $60.

....ARD WEBSTER (England)

The maker's name on the bottom of these teapots is nearly unreadable with age and use. Only the last three letters of the first name can be read. Possibilities: Leonard, Richard, Millard, Willard. Several English potteries had, and still have, the last name Webster. We found only two examples with this mark, both identical teapots except for painting variations. They turned up thousands of miles apart—one in England, the other in Southern California, both with undeciferable backstamps. Probably from the 1930s.

337 and 338. **...ard Webster** Two teapots, 5" high, identical in shape and coloring. Knobby relief, brown, yellow, green, white. Mark, "...ard Webster Anne Hathaway's Cottage Made in England." £40. $65.

WEISS (United States)

339. **Weiss** Cookie jar, 10 ½" high. Round beige castle with turreted pink tile roof. Yellow, blue, and rust muted colors. Marked "Weiss Hand Painted in Brazil." £22.$35

WESTERN GERMANY

A tea, coffee, or luncheon set, service for five, are all marked "Made in Western Germany," with an incised design mark. It is easy to date. The mark was used from 1945 until 1992, when the division of Germany into east and west zones ended and the dividing Berlin Wall came down. Pieces are painted in glowing shades of golden yellow and brown, with pine cone accents. A different architectural design than English cottage ware.

Western Germany base marking

340. **Western Germany** Teapot, 7 1/2" high Straight sides, dark green handle and spout, yellow and brown thatched roof. £45. $55.

341. **Western Germany** Cup and Saucer. £19. $23.

342. **Western Germany** Coffeepot, 7" high. Dark green handle and spout, yellow and brown thatched roof. £28. $40.

343. **Western Germany** Plates, 7 1/2" diameter. £7. $10 each.

344. **Western Germany** Creamer, 3" high. Dark green handle. £19. $25.

345. **Western Germany** Covered Sugar, 4" high. Yellow and brown thatched roof, dark green handles £18. $23.

346. **Western Germany** Cups and Saucers. £13. $20 set.

WESTERN HOUSE GIFTS (United States)

Western House Gifts, probably a distributor of novelty ware. No information found, except that marked on the bottom of the teapot.

347. **Western House Gifts** Teapot, 7" high. Pub with sign "The Crown" in front. Grey and white with dark brown outlines. Rose colored brick chimney, and flowers. Marked "The Village Collectables" and "Village Ware." £20. $30.

348. **Westminster** Covered Butter Dish, 4 1/2" high on 6 1/2" long tray with thatched edge. Tiered thatched roof, browns, greenery, white windows. £45. $85.

WESTMINISTER (England)

Westminister Pottery Ltd was located in Hanley, and part of Staffordshire Potteries, from 1948 - 1956, They produced earthenware pieces, and introduced a variety pieces, including cottage ware. All pieces shown have similar colorings and design.

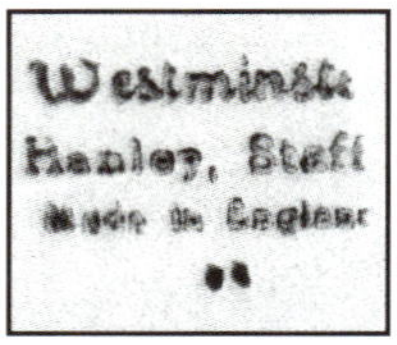

Westminster
base marking

349. **Westminster** Teapot, 5 1/2". £35. $65.

350. **Westminster** Covered Butter Dish, 4 1/2" high on 5 1/2" long tray with thatched edge. Tiered thatched roof, browns, greenery, white windows. Same as #351. £45. $75.

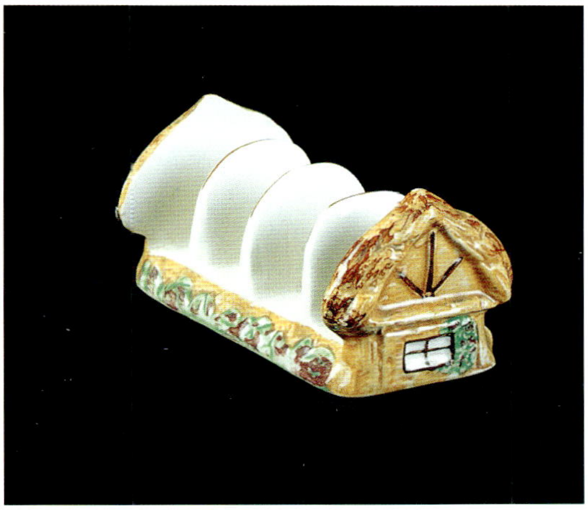

351. **Westminster** Toast Rack, 4-slice, 2 1/4" high, 4 1/2" long. £30. $65.

352. **Westminster** Footed Egg Cups (4) on squared cloverleaf tray with inserts for cups. Cups, 2 1/4" high. Tray, handle to handle, 7" long. £35. $95.

ARTHUR WOOD (England)

This company began in 1885 as Copper & Wood, Bradwell Works, Longport. Part of Staffordshire Potteries, they made earthenware pieces, mainly teapots. After 1928, they were known as Arthur Wood & Son Ltd. The backstamp from 1934 was a world globe with a banner. This was altered in 1945, and again in 1954. Reference books do not show the mark on the teapot pictured here, which may mean it was made before the 1958 shown in reference books.

Arthur Wood base markings

353. **Arthur Wood** Biscuit Barrel, 6 1/2" high to top of handle. Square, three-story, cream, brown, green. Green and brown long tray with thatched edge. Tiered thatched roof, browns, wrapped straight handle. £60. $125.

354. **Arthur Wood** Teapot, 5 1/2" high. Three-story, matches #349 biscuit barrel. Cream, brown, green. £55. $95.

TONY WOOD Studios (England)

A number of English potters, many famous, have the name of Wood. Several can be found under Wood & Son or Wood & Sons. Tony Wood could be a descendent of a family of potters; it is a fairly common name. The backstamp gives no indication of where or when the firm operated. The teapot shown appears to be from the 1950s.

Tony Wood Studio
base marking

355. **Tony Wood Studio** Teapot, 5" high. Dark green, highly glazed, gray-blue, relief figures in front. Darker colors than most. Marked "Tony Wood Made in England." £35. $95.

Glossary

Art Deco - The period in time of the 1920s to the 1940s, the time span when most cottage ware was produced

Back Stamp - Maker's mark usually on back or bottom of a ceramic piece. Also usually includes country of origin, required by U.S. law for imported goods. Intended to protect U.S. manufactured goods, since there is a tariff on imports. No identification required on wares intended for domestic use, not export.

Biscuit Barrel - A lidded container for storing cookies, which the British call biscuits.

Butter Box - A box with a lid on it, rectangular in shape, for storing butter

Butter Dish, covered - Could be round, square, or rectangular. A flat dish or tray with a top that is large enough to cover a quantity of butter. The finial is usually in the middle. Larger ones are commonplace in England. In the U.S., the usual sized butter dish will cover a cube of butter or margerine.

Cheese Dish, covered - These are made to cover a wedge of cheese. The top is usually slanted to allow for the shape. Larger than a butter dish, with funial higher for balance

Coffee Pot - Differs from a Teapot in that the spout doesn't extend down to the bottom of the pot, and it is usually taller, with straight sides.

Cold Painted - Painted after the glaze has been fired.

Condiment Set - Usually 3 pieces (salt, pepper, mustard) plus tray and mustard lid.

Cottage Ware - Originally dishes and household pieces intended for use in a cottage, but now refers to dishes and household pieces shaped like cottage or other dwelling.

Creamer/Jug - A creamer (for coffee) is usually smaller than a jug intended to hold milk for tea (in England), or if covered, hot water. The word jug is more common in England.

Egg Cup - A ceramic cup designed to hold the bottom half of a boiled egg to make eating it easier. The top half of the egg is exposed, making it simple to cut the shell. The egg is eaten out of the bottom half which remains intact.

Encised Mark - Cut into the piece before firing

Finial - Lid top of jar or pot, for lifting lid

Glaze - A glossy finish on ceramics or china.

Half-Timbered - Timber or wood which protrudes on a plastered or stuccoed building, usually on the top half of the building. Half of the building is then timbered, hence half-timbered.

Honey Pot - Same as Jam Pot, but frequently with relief bees somewhere on the pot or as a finial on lid

Impressed Mark - Cut into the piece before firing

Jam/Marmalade Pot - Lids have an opening for the spoon

Jar, Pot, Container, Storage Jar, or Canister - All more or less exchangeable words to describe a kitchen or table container

Kiln - Cone-shaped oven for firing pottery

Lithophane - A porcelain panel with varying layers of thickness to allow light to show through.

Match Holder -Ceramic holder with an open space to hold matches for fireplace. Usually has a roughened area for striking.

Mill - A common theme in cottage ware. Most farming villages had a mill near a water supply, to grind grain to produce flour.

Muffin Dish - Covered. A plate with a round cover, to accommodate one or two muffins and keep them warm.

Pastille - French for pill

Pastille Burner - A container with an opening to hold a perfumed pill which is burned to disguise unpleasant odors. Similar to an incense burner.

Pot Bank - A century or so ago, potters lived in a pot bank, a dwelling that also included a kiln and a work area.

Pub - Common in England, so called because it is a Public House, found in every village, a social gathering place that serves beer, ale, other spirits, and snacks.

Pitcher/Jug - Americans usually use the word Pitcher to describe a pouring container, but in England these are called Jugs.

Slip - Webster's definition is slime or slime paste. This diluted clay is applied to a completed clay or porcelain piece before firing, to produce a glossy finish.

Shaker - Has perforated top for salt, pepper, or sugar. Sugar shakers are usually taller, with many holes.

Thatch - an old-time roof found on cottages, made of hay or straw on a support of branches.

Transfer design - An applied paper design used as decoration on china, pottery or porcelain before the final firing. Applied in a similar fashion as a decal is today.

Bibliography

AA Illustrated Guide to Britain. Drive Publications Limited, for the Automobile Assn, Basingstoke, Hants, RG 21 2EA England

Busby, Eileen Rose. *Royal Winton Porcelain; Ceramics Fit for a King*, The Glass Press, Marietta, Ohio, 1998.

The Glass and China Trader, England. April 1913, May 1913, August 1913, November 1913, August 1916.

Godden, Geoffrey. *An Encyclopedia of British Pottery and Porcelain Marks*, London, England: Herbert Jenkins Ltd., 1964

Hawley, T. "Sketches of Pottery Life and Character." Staffordshire, England.

Hughes, Bernard and Therle. *The Collector's Encyclopedia of English Ceramics*, London, England. Abbey Library, 1967.

McCoy, Elin. "Tea, It's Just the Cure" *Reader's Digest Magazine*, June 1997.

Miller, Muriel, *Collecting Royal Winton Chintz*, London, England: Francis Joseph, 1998.

Price Guide to Majolica, Gas City, Indiana: L-W Book Sales and Publishing, 1997.

The Royal Winton International Collector's Chintz Newsletter. Dancer's End, Northall, England.

Warner, Ian and Mike Pasgay: *The World of Wade Collectable Porcelain and Pottery*; Antique Publications, Marietta, Ohio.